CLOUDBURST
OF A
THOUSAND SUNS

THE VAANI OF
SRI SRI SITARAMDAS OMKARNATH

Originally Compiled by
TRIDANDI SWAMI MADHAVA RAMANUJA JEEYAR

Rendered in English by
RAJ SUPE
Kinkar Vishwashreyananda

CELESTIAL
BOOKS

ISBN 978-93-81115-62-6
First Published by Jai Guru Sampradaya, Delhi, 2008

Cover Design   Aniruddha Mukherjee
Layouts   Ajay Shah
Printing   Repro India Ltd, Navi Mumbai

Published in India 2011 by
CELESTIAL BOOKS
an imprint of
LEADSTART PUBLISHING PVT LTD
Trade Centre, Level 1
Bandra Kurla Complex
Bandra (E), Mumbai 400 051, INDIA
T + 91 22 40700804
F + 91 22 40700800
E info@leadstartcorp.com
W www.leadstartcorp.com

US Office
Axis Corp
7845 E Oakbrook Circle
Madison, WI 53717, USA

CONTENTS

FOREWORD

Sri Sri Gurave Namah

The *Vaani*, or Gospel of *Yuga Purusha* Ananta Sri Sitaramdas Omkarnath, derives from His personal experiences, gained in the course of a life-long and continual spiritual practice. It has been made available in the form of some small and some voluminous books, and hundreds of letters, journals and periodicals, all calculated to achieve the welfare of mankind. He adds force to his spiritual experiences with the help of wisdom well-versed in the *Shastras*. The bouquets and garlands of his writings are conspicuous by the rare synthesis of scriptural learning and spiritual attainment – *Shabdaarthau iva samyuktau* (blended together like the word and its meaning).

However, there is a dearth of both time and competence, to thoroughly pursue all the collected works and letters of Sri Sitaramdas Omkarnath, stretching indeed to vast proportions. But to cross over to the other shore of spirituality, we have no other way than the companionship of the precious garland of Thakur Omkarnath's gospel.

Having deliberated upon this, Sri Sitaramdas Omkarnath's constant companion and worthy heir of his spiritual treasure, and universally revered, the late Tridandi Swami Madhava Ramanuja Ji Maharaj, dived deep into the ocean of Sri Sri Thakur's spiritual compositions like an adept and brought out a thousand rare gems and pearls, each extremely apt and beneficent. These are published as *Cloudburst Of A Thousand Suns*. I hope, with Swamiji's benign and benevolent efforts, all spiritual aspirants will find the most difficult spiritual path scattered with thorns become easy and strewn with flowers.

It is only after great deliberation that the host of Arya *rishis* described the difficult path of spirituality in the words, *Kshurasya dhara nishita duratyaya*.[1] This path is undoubtedly deep and intricate, but it's not impassable. Its call is irresistible and has been attracting devotees, age after age, to renounce everything and answer the summons. Seekers of all times are known to have stepped out with deep longing in quest of the Supreme. Those who were unable to find the ultimate have secluded themselves behind closed doors, in the lonely precincts of temples or monasteries, or uninhabited banks of rivers and sat down in meditation with great longing for the Supreme. In the lives of even those who could not do this; those who were forever caught in the complex tangle of worldly existence, those who never felt the slightest desire to propitiate God, even in their hearts, at some propitious moment, a cry has arisen that can best be expressed in the words:

---

1 'Like the sharp edge of a razor is that path difficult to cross and hard to tread – thus say the wise.' *Kathopanishad*

Hethaa noy, hethaa noy
Anyo kothaa – Anyo kono khaane…
Not hither, not hither
somewhere else, in some other abode…
~ **Rabindranath Tagore**

These words epitomize the eternal misfit who is in constant search of his/her abode and perhaps never finds it on earth. The heart finds not the abode of the Self anywhere here…it longs to discover its true destination. That's the reason this cry is an eternal cry. Just as the authorities on spirituality have classified the seekers into four categories: lowly, average, advanced and superlative; evaluating the degree of their longing and their individual state, or the hierarchies of disciples, the preceptors have offered different types of counsel.

Their advice to the common householder will surely differ from that offered to a *brahmachari*; there is similarly a difference in counsel to the renunciate. Thus, even on the face of it, it is clear that even a practical minded person will find that Swamiji, with his keen intellect, has carefully divided the *Omkarsahasravaani* text into different headings such as 'The Ground of Spirituality', 'Human Birth & Its Import', 'Nature of Guru', 'Guru *Mantra*', 'Guru Protocol', 'Nature of *Mantra* & *Japa* Ego', 'Me & Mine, Refuge/ Surrender', 'the state of *Kundalini* awakening' etc. *'Food is the foundation of all spirituality. Bhojan* (dietary control) *is inextricably interlinked to Bhajan* (worship).' This is Thakur's *Mahavakya* (great scriptural edict). By merely taking recourse to pure, *sattvik* food, one can succeed in attaining to the eternal reminiscence of the divine. That is the reason one notices that Swamiji has covered purification of diet extensively.

After crossing over the inaccessible waters of spirituality, characterized by inexplicable blows and counter blows, strife within and without, crests and troughs, hope and despair; incomparable service to the Guru together with rigorous asceticism, have helped him come closer to the goal. Madhava Swamiji Maharaj is a *Siddha* who has been a companion, nay an eternal companion, of the world-sanctifying and divine sport of *Nitya Siddha* Sri Sitaramdas Omkarnath. Thus, along with constant endeavour toward the welfare of all beings and severe austerities, excellent study of scriptures has never left his side. No wonder he has a perfect understanding of both, the principal impediments to spirituality, as also the methods of overcoming them. But naturally, he lays emphasis on *Naam* above everything else. The chapter entitled *Naam*, is therefore a testimony of the supreme refuge. Whether it's a *bhakta* or *jnani*; *yogi* or *bhogi*; a *brahmachari* or a householder; a sinner or a saint, *Naam* is the supreme recourse for all and sundry.

Consider the following:

'Keep chanting Naam *always, and blow away the frenzied tensions of the mind, and difficulties on the path of spirituality, with the help of the* Naam-*cannon.'*

14

'Ananda (bliss) is in one's own fist. Name of God is nothing but bundled mass of ananda; there's as much bliss in store for the Naami (chanter) as he chants it.'

'Naam is the wish-yielding tree. Whatever you desire of it, you will get it. You will surely get it. If anyone sings Naam with one wish in mind, a hundred are fulfilled.'

"Sadhan, bhajan etc. are not mere mental concepts; they are not figments of imagination. There is unbounded joy in sadhan and bhajan; they liberate one from old age and death."

We are astounded to observe how revered Swamiji has, for the most part, compiled Sri Sitaramdas Omkarnath's advice pertinent to the common mass of people. For those who are excellent among seekers and absorbed in abstract meditation, we find in the repository of Swamiji an account of the remarkable internal world of Divine Light and Divine Sound accessed exclusively by those who have entered the sanctum.

'When the Kundalini (Serpent Power) is activated, unbroken Naad (Divine Sound) goes on; it is beyond the powers of the spiritual aspirant to stop its momentum. Naad Brahma (Absolute in the form of Sound) sports sometimes in higher and sometimes lower (spiritual centres of the body).'

'When the spiritual aspirant forsakes all company and dwells in solitude, at that time Naad (Divine Sound) manifests in

15

varied aspects. Whether the seeker listens to it or not, the Sound does not cease! Sometimes the (rumbling of) *clouds, sometimes the (humming of) the bee, sometimes (chugging of) the engine, sometimes (gurgling of) the waterfall and sometimes (intoning of)* 'Jai Guru', *or* 'Om Guru' *or* 'Guru Guru' – *she plays in this manner.'*

Just as spiritual aspirants are of different orders, so are the preceptors. Deliverer of this age, Sri Thakur Ramakrishna, fond of parables, classified the (spiritual) physicians, who can help cure the malady of worldly existence, into three categories: lowly, middling and excellent. Even in practical life one observes that a lowly physician asks the patient to have the medicine and goes home; the middling one shelters and entreats the patient repeatedly; but the excellent physician shoves the medicine down the patient's throat, he does not rest until he has ensured that the patient has had it.

Sri Sitaramdas Omkarnath belongs to the category of excellent preceptors, which is why we find, when it comes to spiritual and devotional practices, religious regulations and restraint and related issues, he is a puritan and such a strict disciplinarian. He never shirks away from pointing out the harsh truths that could be in the long-term welfare of the spiritual aspirant.

Hence we find in *Omkarsahastravaani (Cloudburst Of A Thousand Suns)*, a stern and relentless aspect Sitaram. We discern in the words of this composition of Sri Sitaram's gospel, a note of rebuke, and sometimes love and affection mixed with scorn and sarcasm; he roars every now and then, but despite all this, the seasoned spiritual aspirant is only benefitted, for he enjoys at any rate, the unblinking and benign glance of the Supreme Being whose love knows no bounds.

Dharma ki jai ho, Adharma ka nash ho!,[2]
Praniyon men sadbhavana ho!
Vishwa ka kalyan ho!

Kinkar Vitthal Ramanuja
President, Akhil Bharat Jai Guru Sampradaya
Mahamilan Math, Kolkata

---

2 'Let there be victory of *Dharma* over *Adharma*, let there be harmony among all living beings and welfare of the whole world.'

INTRODUCTION

BHUUH

Thousand is a sacred number. In the *RigVedic* hymn on Primal Man ~ *Purusha-Sukta*, we hear of a thousand-headed, thousand-eyed, thousand-footed, primal person who spread all over the world and exceeded it by ten fingers. The so-called non-Vedic *Dravida Veda* of Nammalvar, the low-caste Shathakopa, the first teacher of our Sri Sampradaya lineage, consists of a thousand heart-melting songs about Krishna. These thousand Tamil songs are called *Thiruvaymodi*. In Sanskrit, these songs were loved by both our divine speaker Sri Sri Thakur, as well as by Srimat Madhava Ramanuj Jeeyar Swami, our compiler. We were instructed by Sitaram to recite the thousand names of Vishnu daily. And thanks to M.S. Subbalakshmi, the recorded version of those beautiful names of the Lord now reverberates throughout southern India in numerous temples and households.

But the most mystically important place where the secret of a 'thousand' is preserved inside our body, is right on top of our brain. The chain of six lotuses strung together by the subtle energy-channel, called the holy sonorous *sushumna*[1], is crowned by the thousand-petalled *Sahasrara*. This is a special lotus with a thousand white petals, where the Guru sits, embracing his *Shakti* to his left.

With each of these ten hundred memorable messages of our Sri Guru, we could consecrate each of these petals of the lotus in our cranium. In a verse of *RigVeda*, X.164, quoted copiously by Sitaram in his writings and speeches, where the *Vedic verbum* – *gaurir mimaaya salilam...* is described most explicitly, from one, two, three four, or more, twenty-four syllables (of *Gayatri*), the extent of cosmic speech is announced. The limit of that description is in a metre – a syllabic syntax – which is said to be of a 'thousand-syllables' in the Supreme Sonic Space. May these thousand messages of our Master Omkarnath, resonate in the space of our hearts in that cosmic rhythm of 'sahasrakshara vaak' in *param vyoma*.

BHUVAH

Many of these messages are culled from the Master's writings, although they could often be heard rolling out from his mouth too. Most vividly do I remember that mouth which spoke or read out these original words in Bengali! Those lips were thin, nearly invisible under the silky white facial hair. Thin and slightly upturned, the lower lip would start quivering sometimes with infinite

---

1 *Sushumna* is a *Naadi* in the human subtle body. It is one of the body's main energy channels that connects the base *chakra* to the crown *chakra*.

love for Mother Durga, or Sri Krishna or Sri Rama. Sometimes it would be firmly pursed when he would assume the first person and thunder forth:

'Do not imagine distinctions between what is possible and what impossible for Me! I can tie an elephant with the fibre of a lotus-stem. I can drown a mountain in the puddle made by a cow's hoof! Just chant my name, and I shall save you. Fear not, from sin, from death, disease, poverty or the scary cycle of rebirths. I am there for you, I am yours, I am there, My dear!'

This was his 'fiery assurance' – the fireworks of fearlessness spurting out of the most delicate pair of lips, crafted as it were, for only playing the flute.

And when it came to writing, those small frail-looking, tender hands, gripped the pen in a firm but worshipful offering pose. Here, I am torn between two incompatible similes for the words which would issue forth from that blessing-blossoming right hand of our tireless writer. Some of those words were like sharp arrows flying straight to the target, while some were delicate exquisite flowers making us, their addressees, feel really like images of God, as he would call us – *Sribhagavad Virgaha*[2]! Or should I mix the metaphors and call them 'flower-arrows', for indeed, which Love-god could compete with the sureness with which Sitaram's love would take aim at our poor, unworthy hearts?

---

2 Embodiment of God

As Sitaram would answer thousands of complaining, beseeching, pestering, hurting, quarreling letters, in hand-writing like rows of pearls, his head – crowned with masses of matted hair – would bend down in perfect pin-pointed concentration over the sheet of paper, his left hand lovingly hugging the corner of the desk. He would be so lost in the act of writing that even the slightest breathing on his shoulder or a faintest noise next to him would startle him nearly to a jump, though his annoyance would soon melt away into a self-mocking giggle. Brief, to-the-point, humane, and deep, those written letters would often contain gems of wisdom, later collected by Srimat Madhav Swamijee in a different collection (*AThousand Letters of Omkar*). Not just at the time of daily letter-writing service ('*patra-seva*' as he termed it), even during his long yearly stretches of vows of silence, out of his pen would flow not just streams, and waterfalls, but full oceans of time-transcending written divine elixir of life. Some sun-kissed waves of those seas of writing are translated here by Raj Supe aka Kinkar Vishwashreyananda.

In the original title of these collected messages, *vaanii*, we must realize, covers both oral and inscribed words. So, as we read them, even in translation, we should imagine also hearing them, especially as the Names of God – Ram, Krishna, Hari, Shiva, Durga, Kaali, Narayana – are woven together in many of these messages with their *mantra*-like potency that, through the reader's phonetic imagination, could 'enter straight into the heart through the doors of the ear'. *Shruti*, after all is 'to be heard, reflected upon, and then meditated on.'

In his *Abhaya-vaanii* (translated as 'Hope Abounding'), Sitaram described himself, not as an author but as a scribe (*lipikara*). He would literally 'hear' these authorless words, sometimes in the unstruck sound rising from his heart, the unforgettable words of Krishna in the *Bhagavad Gita*: 'Yada, yada hi dharmasya glanir bhavati Bhaarata!' for example, and would simply write them down for us.

So, just as his works do not make him a worker ('kartaram api mam, viddhi a-kartaram' ~ *Bhagavad Gita*), doing so much he remains a non-doer, his books do not make him an author. His sentences remain authorless *shruti*.

SVAH

One of the running themes of Sri Sri Sitaramdas Omkarnath's philosophy is: that the Name and the Named are One. For a few moments, therefore, let us meditate on the name of the original author of these authorless sentences. What an uncommon name it is!

Sitaramdas Omkarnath! What is the secret of this co-presence of *daas* (servant) and *naath* (master)? What does Sitaram have to do with Omkar? A name like 'Sitaramdas', by itself is quite common in the Ramanuja-

Ramananda lineage (*sampradaya*), marking Vaishnava bhakti, servitude, and surrender to Sita and Rama. And a name like Omkarnath – originally a name given to Sri Sri Thakur by Swami Dhruvananda Giri, of the *Shankarite Advaita* tradition – is understandable from the opposite *jnana*-centered point of view of *Advaita Vedanta*. But their combination is not just rare; it is unique. It breaks age-old barriers and transcends divisions between *Jnana* and *Bhakti*, *Vaishnava* and *Shaiva*, self-humbling and self-expansion. It is by being a humble slave of Sri Sitaram, incarnated in the name Sitaram, that Thakur attains the spiritual height of recognizing his intrinsic identity with *Omkara*.

There is a grammatical trick with which, in one place of his writings, Thakur interprets Omkarnath as: 'One whose Lord is Omkar'. But here and there, we get hints that even the straightforward interpretation: 'The Lord of Omkar', is meant by Thakur when he assumes that name. There are messages in this book which explain briskly how the path of repeating the Name of the Divine, leads one from servitude of God to complete non-dual merging with God and even to a status beyond the audible *Om*, into a sound beyond sound, self beyond self – a state which can be described as 'Mastery over *Omkar*'. Hence the two parts of the name, though apparently incompatible, fuse into one.

MAHA

Some major themes from the text of these messages are:

o Spirituality for the crisis of *Kali Yuga*
o Human birth and death
o Fragility of life
o Goal of life
o The search within
o Need for resolve and optimism
o No need to renounce this world
o What is *dharma*?
o Knowledge
o Devotion
o Non-duality
o Depression versus dispassion
o Essence of spiritual practice
o Practice of God's omnipresence
o Suffering is auspicious
o Perils of fault-finding
o Essential oneness of all: reason for not criticizing
   others
o Sufficiency of chanting the name of God (*Naam*)
o Power of *Naam*
o Divine Name satisfies all desires
o Not a single *Naam* is lost

And so on.

Of course, at the heart of it all is Thakur's central teaching of the simple two-fold path: of repeating the Name and bowing down to everything, living and non-living, treating them as God or Guru.

JNANA

We must say a few words about the compiler. For more
than 25 years, Kinkar Omananda was literally the closest
monastic disciple of Sitaramdas Omkarnath. He followed
him like a shadow, taking care of the Master's frail frame,
cooking all his meals… and of course, cooking for Sitaram
meant, on an average, cooking for hundreds daily, reading
out scriptures under the Master's guidance in the
afternoon reading sessions. But somehow, through this
stormy routine of sleepless work under the cyclonic
Omkarnath, Omananda managed to practice the severest
of concentrated *japa* and *tapasya*. He received the esoteric
inner initiation in the supreme *mantra, Om*, which is called
brahmi diksha. Later on, in Srirangam, in 1976, the Master
arranged for him to be formally ordained as a
Tridandiswami (a holy master with a three-stick staff), of
the Ramanuja order, when his name was changed to
Sriman Madhav Ramanuja Jeeyar Swami. He has been
an author of Sri Sitaramdas Omkarnath's memoirs and
biography in his own right.

TAPAH

Sitaram's relationship with his own spiritual teacher was
a strange one. Himself a very witty, refined, musical, poet
in Sanskrit, his teacher Srimad Dasharathi Dev Yogeshwar
was not only a famous teacher of scripture and rituals, he
was also an advanced *yogin* and a devotee of Lord Krishna.
But the teacher himself was puzzled about who his
mysterious young disciple was. Dasharathidev called
Prabodh (Sitaram's given name at birth), his younger

brother, his friend, his disciple, and also his advisor. In an inspired Sanskrit verse, Dasharathi asked Sitaram: 'I don't know if you are my teacher or my pupil. If you are my preceptor, then I am taking refuge in you as a humble disciple, please teach me. If you are my pupil, then tell me what are you made of?'

We shall try to understand the historical background of Sitaram's own thousand-faced philosophy, in the light of three simple assurances or messages that his teacher Dasharathi once wrote down for him. For the rest of his life, on each occasion of advising people in distress, Sitaram would recall these three messages.

The three *vaanis* of his own Guru that Sitaram used to recite and re-write countless times were:
1. 'The world is subject to change (*jagat paribartanshil*).'
2. 'Such days will not persist (*aisa din nehi rahega*).
3. 'What the supreme Lord of the world does is for the good (*jagadishwar ja koren mangaler janya*).
So, how to stick to the original intent, without slipping into repetitiveness?

I have worried about this for many years. I would suggest, now, that we take all three statements to be warnings against three varieties of *rajas* – *rajoguna* – functions. Remember the *Gita* (recalled in *Sudhar Dhara*): the two inner enemies of man are *kama* and *krodha*, both *rajo-guna samudbhava*.

1. Overpowered by *sattva*-mixed *rajas*, a person perceives the world as full of frustration and suffering and begins to blame his destiny, his own past *karma*, and God, for making his life such hell. To such a person – who is proud of his intellect (*sattva*) and is plagued by pure anguish of intellectually analyzing life and finding it empty of any joy, the cautioning message of optimism is: 'Whatever the world-ruler God does, is for our own Good (happiness + virtue), who are you to think that you understand it all, when you cannot know how much goodness/happiness all this evil/pain is going to lead to? (*Jagadjishwar ja koren monagaler janya*).' This cheers up and gives us hope.

2. Overpowered by *rajas*-mixed-*rajas*, the success-drunk, arrogant, enterprising, restless constant wealth-gatherer thinks: (as described in the 16th chapter of the *Gita*): 'I am the best, look at my achievements, no one will ever be equal to or better than me, the world is in my control!' To such a person, the second message says: 'The world tends to reverse fortunes, it works like the rolling wheel, the up goes down, and the down comes up (*Jagat paribartanshil*).' *Paribartan* in Sanskrit literally means 'going round in a cycle'. So, this does the opposite job, shatters overconfidence and makes the proud humble.

3. Overpowered by *tamas*-mixed-*rajas*, the fatigued, bored, zestless seeker says: 'O well! What's the point

of trying anything? It has always been the same, one day is the same as another, this mixture of wisdom and folly, of pleasure and pain, evil and good is it just going to continue for ever? So why bother?' To such a deluded loser, the third message says: 'Prepare yourself for a surprise, such a day as today is not going to last, something new, something dramatically different may happen, so don't give up, keep up your effort, miracles do happen (*Aisa din nehi rahega*).'

SATYAM ~ the Bottom Line
When Thakur would end a written message addressed to one of us, he used a variety of signature styles. Formally, in early life, he used to sign with a flourish as 'Sri Sitaramdas Omkarnath, servant of the servant of Bhgavan Dasharathi Dev'. But later on, he experimented with informal and simpler formulations such as, 'Yours Sitaram' and 'Yours Omkar'. Sometimes, in a deep intimate and suggestive way, he would end the letter with, 'Yours I' (*Tor ami*). The signal was that his relation to the addressed person was one of total oneness; he was the self of the person he was writing to. But once, going even further into the depths of the wonder that is the Self, he ended a note to someone in a mysterious, endearing, tantalizing fashion:

> *Iti, tor bol dehi ke?*
> (That's all for now,
> Yours Tell Me Who?)

As we read these thousand jewels of love and wisdom, let us meditate on these two personal signatures: 'Yours I' and 'Yours Tell Me Who?'

Let the Master of Omkar, through his vibrant messages, make us servants of Sitaram, sucking us back into his ubiquitous self-essence, and thereby awaken in us the most blissful inquiry of all: 'Tell me who am I?'

Dr Arindam Chakrabarti
Professor of Philosophy, University of Hawaii

1

THE GROUND OF SPIRITUALITY

1. O those intent on self-development, awake, arise –
    you are a human being and not an animal! Awake!
    Arise! Stake your whole life and march forward along
    the path shown by the *Shastras*[1] with your heart and
    soul. Chant *Naam*[2] and go on – may your path be
    strewn with flowers! *Jai Guru!*

2. For all beings, there is but One Master who is the Soul
    of all souls; the Life of his or her life, the Mind of all
    minds, the Eye of all eyes. As long as He is not known,
    one has to undergo distress and suffering, sorrows
    and torment. There is only one way to be liberated
    from infirmity and death and that is to take refuge
    with Him.

---

1 Religious texts or scriptures
2 *Tarak Brahma Naam* viz. *Hare Krishna Hare Krishna Krishna Krishna Hare
Hare, Hare Ram Hare Ram Ram Ram Hare Hare*

3. Everything in this world is subject to creation, maintenance, and destruction. My Mother, possessing three attributes *Sattva–Rajas–Tamas*[3], is ever prone to transformation. Only Brahma is said to be untransformed – He alone is perpetually immutable.

4. Brahma or the Supreme Being, assumes several forms to perform His divine sport; when He is forgotten due to the influence of *avidya*[4], He comes to be known as Jivatma[5].

5. The ultimate quest of all beings is *moksha* (final beatitude). Everyone is eagerly wishing for *moksha* alone – be it a *jnani*, *yogi* or *bhakta*, everyone is praying constantly for *moksha*.

6. The goal for a *bhakta* is to be established in the knowledge, *Vasudeva sarvam* (i.e. Everything is God). For a *jnani*, the goal is to realize and be rooted in the knowledge, *Aham Brahmasmi* (i.e. I am Brahma).

---

3 In *Samkhya* philosophy, a *guna* is one of three tendencies: *tamas, sattva,* and *rajas*. These categories have become a common means of categorizing behavior and natural phenomena in Hindu philosophy. *Sattva* has been translated to mean balance, order, or purity, associated with uplifting and life-supporting qualities. *Rajas* is translated to mean preservation or dynamism. *Tamas* has been translated to mean too inactive or inertia, negative, lethargic, dull, or slow; associated with darkness, delusion, or ignorance.
4 Metaphysical ignorance
5 Individual soul

7. If you look at the theatrical acts of this world and laugh and cry, how am to blame for that? You have become a king in a dream and you are dancing like a madman. Whose fault is it?

8. Everything is Me – you are merely a witness! Don't cry anymore looking at the drama of life! Don't lament any longer by calling dream a reality! Don't forget even for a moment that you are a witness, you are not the actor – let this be settled.

9. Listen, my dears! You people ran madly to 'this one'[6] and took refuge with me who am your eternal companion, and dear as life! You wanted me to alleviate several torments. See, what your Master has done! Your beloved Lord has established so many *ashrams*[7] and temples to give joy to everyone. He has been calling you: 'Come!' 'Come!' He is calling out in the form of many assemblies singing *Naam* incessantly; numerous books, dozens of periodicals and *Naam* in the streets of this country, can't you hear his call? Why have you turned your face away? Why are you crying? Open your eyes and see! Here is a remedy to dispel your sorrow! Do you know what it is? Nothing but shelter of the Lord who is calling you with outstretched arms! To hold you close to His heart and usher you into the realm of bliss, He gives you a summons. Run to Him! Hurry!

---

6 Sri Sri Sitaramdas Omkarnath
7 Hindu monasteries

10. Three important questions: What is soul? Where does it abide? How can it be realized? Soul is *Jyotirmaya Naad-Atmak Omkar* (cosmic sound made of sound and light). It abides in the heart. It can be realized through *Naad-Anusandhana* (i.e. *Naam Yoga*), or inquiring within one's inner sound.

11. *Pravritti-patha-yaatris*, or those inclined towards the path of action and worldly life, adhere to worship and sacrifices and having obtained *svarga*[8], return to the mortal world, and then again head off to *svarga*. Performing duties in this manner, when the *sattva guna*[9] predominates, they take to the *nivritti* path or the path of renunciation. For those inclined towards *nivritti*, undertaking activities appropriate to one's order, first the mind is purified, then to gain self-knowledge, they take refuge with a *satguru*[10].

12. Human beings come into this world in order to realize God, if this object is sidelined and the heart longs only for sense gratification, then it is inevitable that the next life will either be that of an animal or an immoveable object. There is no path to the knowledge of God except through the renunciation of sense enjoyment.

---

8 Heavenly region
9 Mode of purity, intellect and goodness
10 A self-realized Master, embodiment of righteousness

13. The sense organs like the eyes, ears, nose etc., are madly and rapidly being drawn towards their natural objects such as form, sound, smell, touch, taste etc. This is not the spiritual ordain of life, it can only be called death. The *rishis*[11] of the past have left us an easy course through which one can conquer life while performing one's daily duties.

14. Even the learned scientists of the day haven't been able to get hold of the genuine truth underlying nature. My dear, is nature everything? Do you think the play of nature is all? *Prakriti*[12] isn't everything; she is merely a partner in the divine play.

15. As long as a man is interested in sense enjoyment and material pleasure, he stays away from ascetic practices and the precepts of *dharma*.

16. Just as if you were to say 'I obey my father', but don't heed his advice in practice, it does not constitute true obedience to one's father; similarly, mere verbal claim of allegiance to God without praying at appropriate hours, only amounts to disloyalty to Him.

17. If listening to just one thing resulted in knowledge of Brahma, there would be a *Brahma-jnani*[13] in every house.

---

11 Hindu seers
12 Primordial Nature, which in association with Purusha, creates the universe.
13 Knower of ultimate truth

18. People who are ardently longing for worldly enjoyment and casting aspersions at the *Shastras* (scriptures)! Alas! They know not; they don't have the slightest idea of the poison they are drinking. How much suffering lies in store for them! They will all suffer night and day.

Kali Yuga–Kali Dharma ~ Crisis of the Present Times

19. At present Kali[14] reigns supreme with its terrible dance. Almost everyone is walking on a path opposed to the scriptures and suffering distress. Far-sighted *rishis*, versed in the past, present and future, had already documented in the scriptures that things would come to such a pass.

20. With the winds of West, good things like profound customs, virtuous conduct, faith and devotion have gone astray. The children of *Bharatamata* (Mother India) have lost their character and deteriorated over the last three or four generations.

21. You are looking at the prosperity of Western civilization as though you are seeing a dream world! You are seeing it as if you are looking through a *bioscope*! But what is it to you?

---

14 Kali, the male demon, presiding over *Kali Yuga* (lit. age of Kali or age of vice). It is the last of the four stages that the world goes through as part of the cycle of *yugas* described in the Indian scriptures.

22. The current crisis can only be settled through adherence to *dharma*. The fire that is burning cannot be put out with fire; if the cloud of *dharma* rains down perpetual restraint, then there is a possibility of redemption, otherwise the chances are bleak.

23. The more man is progressing in sophistication and materialism, the more he has abandoned the path laid down by the scriptures; having turned to sense gratification he is encountering disease, misery, sorrow, privation, and suffering.

24. Try to inquire into the present condition of those who have no restraint. They have no power, they cannot conduct themselves virtuously, cannot muster self-discipline. And they reproach the *Shastras* (scriptures). Why? What harm have the scriptures done to you? Have you ever tried to test what is the fruit attained by observing *sandhya*[15] at the prescribed hours?

25. The whole race of men and women of today is in panic – in disease, in sorrow, in distress, in want and suffering. No one has the power to dispel this hue and cry. This fire is raging as a consequence of the downright disregard shown to the *Shastras* (scriptures).

---

15 *Sandhya* means a juncture of time of a day. The word means the ritual worship three times a day, morning, noon and evening at sunrise, midday and sunset respectively.

26. Today the focus is on earning money and that is the cause of the increase in suffering. It is leading human beings astray, towards destruction.

27. Men bereft of the divine touch! You did not come into this world with wife, children, high post and money; when you leave this world, you won't be able to take these with you. When your son gives you *agni* at the last rite, he won't send the money, property, and wealth with you – everything will be left behind. That is why I am telling you to come forward. Come, there is nothing to fear. You won't have to spend money in *Ishta Puja*[16]. Your Beloved does not want any money, any property; all He wants is your heart.

28. Have you ever tried to ascertain the result of a holy dip in the Ganga, devotional service to a *Tulsi*[17] plant, worship of the *Shivalinga* and *Shaligrama*? Have you ever probed as to how a *sattvik* diet improves health? Please try to do it and see for yourself.

The Call

29. Come! Come all of you – men and women burning with the misery of *samsara*[18]! Put an end to the evil deeds of the past through expiation; purify your body and start calling out to God. He will grant you *darshan* (vision); you will win supreme bliss. You will definitely have it.

---

16 Worship of one's favourite deity
17 Holy Basil
18 Worldly existence

30. In every home across India, there is a cry of lamentation. *You* become the ideal – bring floods of joy to their lives.

31. I appeal to you; come! My dear men and women of the Arya race, return back to your *dharma*, to your *karma*, to your *sadhana*[19]! Show deference unto the *Shastras* (scriptures).

32. Come brothers! Come children! Come! Return to your kingdom of peace! You are suffering great torment because of your mindless indulgence in material enjoyment. Return! Return to restraint! Back to your renunciation, your worship, your austerity.

33. This is my call to every Indian, to the amateur and the expert, to anyone who is intent on doing well. Come! Adopt the path of the *Shastras* (scriptures) – good fortune will come your way, the object of your heart will also be realized. You will neither achieve anything by renouncing the *Shastras*, nor can you ever succeed in establishing a new *Shashtra* at any time.

Human Birth & Its Import

34. The *Vedas*, the *Upanishads*, the *Puranas*, the *Tantras*, the *Samhita*, all direct one along the path, following which, one can gain that one *Purusha*[20]. They have laid down different paths for persons with different

---

19 Spiritual practice
20 Supreme Being

qualifications. The aim of every person is to get established in one. All want the 'One' not 'Two'. Some want to be united with Him, some want to mingle in Him – that is the only difference.

35. The human body is not to be acquired without performing virtuous or sinful deeds. As a consequence of virtuous deeds, the desire for spiritual practice is born in you; as a consequence of sin, the mind suffers a fall – but it will lift up again! It is every person's lot to rise and fall in spiritual life, like the ebb and flood tides of the Ganga. The fall only helps in returning with greater determination.

36. One is able to acquire the human body after performing *sadhana*[21] for several lives. The human body is hard-earned. That is why it is the duty of every human being to realize God.

37. Only the life of human beings is controlled by *karmas* performed in previous births. Such is not the prerogative of the animals etc.

38. Human beings are indeed the greatest creations of God because it is only in a human being that God has vested the freedom to exert all the sense organs according to will; God witnesses if this freedom of senses is abused.

---

21 Spiritual practice

39. You have obtained a birth as a human being which is difficult to get; Guru has been kind enough to bestow a *mantra*; you will get whatever you want near the wish-yielding tree of the *mantra*. You shall realize the four-fold objects of *dharma-artha-kaam-moksha*[22] from your *mantra*.

40. The moment a man is born, the state in which he is to leave this world is determined. Nobody has the power to touch a single hair. Death is a singular occurrence; it cannot take place twice.

41. Perform all your tasks from morning till you go bed bearing in mind the fact 'we have come into this world to realize God'.

Life and Death ~ Impermanence

42. Oh, you deluded traveller, how much longer, like a mad man, will you be running about on the wrong path? Tear forcibly the net that ties you to ignorance and delusion and come along with me; you who have lost your way. Now you will have to take a path which you do not know. What fare have you saved in this life for this journey? You gained a life which is difficult even for the gods to attain, but, what a pity you have

---

22 In Hinduism *purushartha* or 'that which is sought by man; human purpose, aim, or end', refers to a goal, end or aim of human existence. *Dharma* – religious, social and/or moral righteousness, both spiritual and ritual; *Atrha* – material and/or financial prosperity as well as pursuit of meaning; *Kama* – sensory and/or sexual pleasure as well as spiritual love; *Moksha* – spiritual liberation or renunciation as well as detachment

wasted such a life in chasing a mirage. So come! Now, come along with me.

43. It is extremely difficult to determine the course of destiny. Destiny can agitate even a person who has seen God.

44. It is no good if you like this world, but it is very good if you find this world no good.

45. This world is like a dream. Wife and children, kith and kin, or even one's own body for that matter, are destined to perish and are impermanent. No one knows who will have to depart and when the call will come. Food, sleep, fear and sex are common to both men and animals – the only thing that differentiates men from animals is *dharma*.

46. We live in a dream world – there is no telling when this dream and happiness will break, only the name of God is true. To take recourse to *Naam* with firm determination, is the only genuine duty of man.

47. In the dream world, in the theatre of life, happiness and sorrow, honour and dishonour, peace and disharmony, dearth and affluence are all actors decked up to act. Appearing one after the other, these destroy (deplete the effect of) our past actions (*karma*).

48. Listen, O Mother! This world is a dream-construct, a mirage! Whatever you see here is untrue. Everything of this world: happiness and sorrow, laughter and tears, torment and sufferings are as untrue as a dream. How sorely do we cry taking the unreality of the world to be true, how we rant and rave! How much we scream! But all this is nothing but a dream.

49. There is no guarantee whether this *samsara*[23] will exist tomorrow or not. So where is the time to laugh and weep and think of its happiness and sorrows, honour and dishonour? Don't worry; pray with all your yearning heart and all things will be taken care of.

50. All the prosperity in the world is destroyed with the advent of time; where there is a rise, the fall too is inevitable; union finally changes into separation and the life of an individual finally reaches destruction.

51. This world is the mine of all manner of sorrows. Undivided happiness or sorrow is not anyone's lot. He, who is seen immersed in immeasurable happiness at present, is suddenly found plunged into the ocean of insurmountable sorrow.

52. The irreligious one spends his days tumultuously, in burning pain, poverty, disease, sorrow and want.

---

23 Worldly existence

53. Men and women who forget their true values in the momentary mist of short-lived youth, and consider gratification of the senses to be the goal of their life, have to undergo untold suffering in the end.

54. Those who take refuge at God's feet: they are the ones whose dream is shattered; they wake up. When they look at the faces of those who cry out deep in their sleep, they feel like laughing. They call them out and say, 'Listen! Don't cry; you are seeing a dream. Wake up! Rise!'

55. Call out to God! Why have you come here? And what are you doing? You basically came into this world to call out to God and then forged relationships in this world, why are you raising an uproar now? You will have to leave this world some day, what solution have you got for that? It is to drive this point home that the awakened one cries himself hoarse.

Death Draws Near

56. We are deluded by our thirst for pleasure and we do not realize that we are sitting on the shores of death. Your lifespan is draining into the ocean of *kala* (time). every second. We do not know when the signal will come for any of us to be taken away by *mahakala*. Then we shall have to discard all hopes and aspirations of pleasure and lie asleep in the lap of death like a quiet child. In the abode of all our hopes, the fire of

44

death will be blazing fiercely. Everything will be left behind – the *samasar*, relatives, wealth, honor, knowledge, pride etc. Your only companion will be the fruits of your work. Taking this accumulated fruit of all work done by you in this life, you will embark on an unknown path with which you are not at all acquainted.

57. There is no telling when and at what time we will have to leave; which is why everyone should try not to let time pass unproductively. The easy path available in *Kali Yuga* is the one of *Naam* and *Leela Chintan*[24]. Chant *Naam*[25]!

58. He who is facing death, what will he care for the pleasures of this world? And why will he be anxious for women or wealth?

59. Death is devouring you every moment, every second! What are you doing about it?

60. He who is travelling towards death, why would he care for the wants of this world? If it comes, well and good! If it doesn't, well and good! Let whatever has to happen ensue; standing or sitting, eating or lying down, just call out to Him.

---

24 Contemplating on the divine sport of the gods
25 *Tarak Brahma Naam* viz. *Hare Krishna Hare Krishna Krishna Krishna Hare Hare, HareRam Hare Ram Ram Ram Hare Hare*

Time is of the Essence

61. The part of life which has passed, one cannot bring back even a moment of it even at the cost of one's life. It is our duty to make our present and past nectar by chanting the Name of God.

62. Try not to waste any time. Whether with reading of scriptures or contemplating God's sport, with *Naam* or with service, keep your mind occupied with any one of these services unto God.

63. The purpose of life is to remember *Hari* (God). Human beings come into this world to realize God. Time is fleeting; the hour of death is drawing close, not just you, every man or woman starts dying from birth itself. Every moment is dragging the human being towards death.

Goal of Life

64. The ultimate goal of every human being is to realize God; everything is here to serve this purpose. Always make sure *satsanga*[26], reading of sacred texts, chanting *Naam* etc., are the backbone of your life. Carry on with your household duties in the spirit that 'this *samsara* (worldly life) belongs to God, I am merely His servant'.

---

26 Company of holy men and the virtuous ones

65. The clarion call has come for all. Come! Do not tarry! My jewel in the crown and my heart's love, come to me! Prepare the provisions for the long journey. Either two hours a day, or two hours a week – each one according to his capability, be blessed by devoting your time in blessed activities such as spreading *Naam* or the holy books or by joining *Naam* celebrations.

66. There is no deed better than impelling a human being towards the path of divinity. All attempts are at work to ensure men and women walk on the right path. One must aid this endeavour. The path of *Naam*[27] is the best by far; it is necessary to let the glorious *Naam Samkirtan* (chanting) continue always.

Inquiry ~ the Search Within

67. Questions arise only in the mind of he who practices spirituality, the rest have no occasion for questions.

68. As long as the human being doesn't dive inside of himself, his miseries do not cease. Calling Him forever and ever, dive deep into yourself.

69. The entire treasure of your spiritual practice forever resides within your own heart, you just have to surrender to it saying, *'Sharanaagatoham* – I am taking refuge with you'*, then there is nothing to worry.

---

27 Chanting the *Mahamantra/Tarak Brahma Naam* viz. *Hare Krishna Hare Krishna Krishna Krishna Hare Hare, Hare Ram Hare Ram Ram Ram Hare Hare*

70. Man can gain boundless happiness by merely turning the mind inwards. The heart of every being is full of sound, light and joy. Curb outside attractions and return to your home.

71. You will reach the kingdom of peace as soon as you are able to contain yourself. Your going out of yourself will only weaken you.

72. Science has introduced only the objects of desire and increased sufferings. Ram! Ram! Peace is not outside. Peace is within. The *mantra* to enter within is repetition of 'Ram', 'Ram'.

73. Science has given rise to terrible darkness; it will not get you anywhere. Science, which grants apparent happiness, has been lauded with a hundred mouths. But O eternally enlightened men of India! This science is not the only thing meant for you. You stand far above this knowledge.

74. Slowly, as the body is purified, the mind begins to turn inwards; the aspirations of the external world go down gradually.

2

THERE'S HOPE

75. Why are you scared? You are a Mother's son, why are you getting a creepy feeling looking at the ghostly dance of the world? All that is untrue – just call out! To date no one has ever failed in realizing their heart-felt wish after taking refuge with God.

76. Don't lose heart. Listen to me! Listen to what I say! Even now it is possible! People who take refuge with God are able to attain peace.

77. Faith in the divine Name is not blind faith. Call Him howsoever you will, call Him, standing, sitting, eating, going to bed – peace shall be yours.

78. As long as there is breath, there is hope. Those who have lost everything, if they call out to God with all their heart, He shows compassion. There is no doubt about this – no doubt whatsoever!

79. If a mighty sinner takes refuge at Guru's feet with exclusive devotion and surrenders to him, he doesn't have to adopt any other spiritual practice.

80. Sorrow, distress, disease, want, debt, happiness, prosperity, applause, ridicule, will continue to bark like dogs in this world; by accepting none of these, and making progress repeating 'Ram', 'Ram', these things will scream and chase you for a while and then become silent automatically.

Determination & Optimism

81. Despite repeated obstructions, excellent men don't forsake the effort they have initiated.

82. There is nothing in this world that cannot be achieved through unflinching perseverance. He who works diligently and with determination, even if he is a paragon of stupidity, with time, he comes to be recognized as a champion among great souls.

83. A stone too wears out when rubbed – one must always bear this fact in mind. Even a person of dull intellect, through perseverance and effort, can realize in time that the subject on hand is not as difficult as it seemed.   Some will grasp it by studying it once, some twice, and some thrice.

84. By dint of repeated effort, anyone can succeed in acquiring the strength that is lacking in himself. 'I am a dull-witted person, how will I achieve this subtle and difficult task?' Reflecting thus and forsaking the task is not a mark of a brave man.

85. Even an easy task becomes difficult to accomplish for a person who thinks, 'I am powerless; how can I accomplish such a difficult task?' For a person with a firm resolve, who, on the contrary thinks, 'I shall surely be able to do this job', even a difficult task is easily accomplished in due course.

86. In point of fact, it is not impossible for any individual to accomplish any object by striving for it, but the lazy ones who are averse to hard work, blame it either on bad luck or their lack of merit and intelligence. They fail to acquire the gem of knowledge and understand the true significance of things.

None Inferior: All are Welcome to His Care
87. Never mind whether you are a sinner or someone in distress, if you are afflicted with disease, or cursed with a thousand offences! Surrender to God saying: 'I have taken refuge with you'. You will surely succeed in securing His Grace. You surely will! There is no doubt about it!

88. One of His names is *Patita Paavana Adhama Taarana* (Uplifter [*lit.* purifier] of the lowly and the fallen ones!); even the greatest of sinner is not precluded from His kindness.

89. No matter how sinful and dissolute a man is – he has nothing to fear if he takes refuge with Him and says from the bottom of his heart, 'God! I am a great sinner, I am degenerate, and I have no hope! Please have mercy on me out of your kindness.' God will lift Him up and clasp him to His heart.

90. Everyone has a right over God. There can be differences of language, some may not have the authority of *Vedic mantras,* but there is no proscription of any kind on love. Everyone can take God captive by means of love.

91. He who is already good, what good can be additionally done to him? However, even if you are able to turn one characterless person towards the path of virtue, enough good is done to the world.

92. If you don't see any hope when you look at yourself, don't lose faith. Believe that He is the redeemer of the sinful! The rescuer of the fallen!

93. No matter which state you are in, the remedy lies in that very condition! Come! Come forward, O you proud of

mortal body! Come forward with the intent of acquiring self-knowledge! Come ye seeker! Come! Step forward on your path. Just serve your Guru. He will absorb you.

94. God is the only support for the devotee. The *yogis* have contemplated upon His feet in solitary places for ages. From those hallowed feet the divine river Ganga, the redeemer of the fallen, and the rescuer of wretches, originates, and sanctifies all the three worlds. No one is despicable. Everyone is supremely pure.

95. To err is human. Being human, there is bound to be some weakness or failing in everyone – thinking thus, one should not reproach anyone – everyone will have to be drawn to one's heart with love.

You Won't Have to Leave this World

96. One constantly hears of renunciation as the first step towards *sadhana*. But there is no need of renunciation. Stay wherever you are and try to chant *Naam* constantly. If you can hold on to *Naam* which is *Bhagawan* Himself, then you need not worry any more. He who stays near the King does not depend on the kindness of the door-keeper. He whose tongue is reluctant to sing *Naam,* may think of renunciation. If one can sing *Naam,* the four types of *sadhana*, i.e. *vivikta* (concentration), *vairagya* (dispassion for the pleasures of this world and of heaven), *mumukshatva* (intense desire for liberation), *shama* and *dama*

(serenity or tranquillity of mind and rational control of the senses), run after him.

97. You won't have to leave this world; you won't have to leave your wife and child; while staying in the midst of them, I will take you to the world of happiness. I will hand you your true nature – look at yourself just once! Why must you be voluntarily bound in attachment? You are free – you have no restriction.

98. It is not necessary to renounce the world; everything is maintained as it is, and one enjoys illimitable pleasure by merely taking refuge with God.

99. In this very life and this very body, you will gain your divine identity – through *sattvik* and pure food, worship at regular hours, *svadhyaya*[1] and daily *japa*.

100. You have slipped down from your divine nature, separated from your real self – that is all! You can re-establish yourself there while continuing to do *japa*. This will be achieved through daily *sadhana*.

101. Experience your true self every day – in the morning, at mid-day and evening prayers. It is not that you will experience and gain something in the distant future. You will obtain supreme happiness right here in this *samsara* and you will be free while staying in the midst of this world.

---

1 Study of Self through introspection and reading spiritual texts etc.

102. If you succeed in living in such a way that you always chant *Naam*[2], you will be free of worldly existence.

103. My dear! One cannot renounce the world by merely talking about it! Renunciation has to be practiced. He who remains within *samsara* and then attempts to undertake *japa* or *dhyana*[3] for one or two hours to begin with, and then about ten to twelve hours, such a person becomes competent to renounce the world. You must practice renouncing *samsara* while staying in the midst of it.

104. Nothing can damage a person more than company or association. While in the company of men, try to look for God. Chant God's Name.

Sanatana Dharma

105. What do you take *Sanatana Dharma*[4] for? Do you think it's fool's play? Nobody has the power to destroy *Sanatana Dharma*. However, this is *Kali Yuga*, and in this age, irreligion is bound to loom large. Sages of yore foretold this long ago.

106. Despite the fact that the influence of *Kali Yuga* has reduced the adherents of *Sanatana Dharma*, no one has the power to destroy it. Even if thousands of wolves form packs, can they devour the lion?

---

2 *Tarak Brahma Naam* i.e. *Hare Krishna Hare Krishna Krishna Krishna Hare Hare, Hare Ram Hare Ram Ram Ram Hare Hare*
3 *Mantra* chanting and meditation
4 Original form of Hinduism, the eternal religion

107. India is the courtyard of *vaikuntha*. Who can banish the Brahmins and the *Shastras* – Sitaram – from here? Rama Rama! Do you know, madcap, that this world is held by these seven:
     1. *Vedas*
     2. *Brahmans*
     3. *Go-mata* (cow)
     4. *Sati* (chaste women),
     5. *Satyavadi* (truthful persons)
     6. *Alobhi* (people free from greed)
     7. *Daansheel* (charitable persons).
     Rama Rama Sitarama! But for these seven, everything would have been a nightmare – Rama Rama!

108. A breed of atheistic and animalistic people, given to impure food habits, devoid of righteousness and purity of conduct, will outrage the *Shastras*[5] and usher in a recalcitrant and heretical religious system. Watch out! Ancient sages have prophesied these things; they will come true – word for word! Never mind! The sway of *Kali Yuga* notwithstanding, *Sanatana Dharma* will protect believers.

---

5 Scriptures

General Duties

109. In the absence of *shaucha*[6] and *sadachara*[7], belief and faith are destroyed, it is impossible to believe there can be anything beyond worldly enjoyments; it is impossible to believe in truths like *jivanmukti, yogamukti, Ishvara*[8] and the eternal veracities of the *Shastras* etc., whatever is done is done wilfully.

110. Take to the service of Guru, service unto God, *Naam kirtan* and prayers thrice a day. Non-violence, truthfulness in speech, internal and external purity, honesty, and control of the senses, are desirable religious duties expected of all. While repeating *Naam*, give yourself up to the care of Sri Gurudeva. You won't have to think of any other duties of birth and clan; you will be full of Guru's import and dwell in delight. Chant:

Hare Krishna Hare Krishna Krishna Krishna Hare Hare
Hare Ram Hare Ram Ram Ram Hare Hare
Sitaram Jai Rajaram, Gauri Shankar Sitaram!
Jai Guru, Jai Naam, Jai Sitaram!

What Is *Dharma*?

111. Food, sleep, fear and sex are common to animals and men. Animals eat, sleep, fear, and enjoy sex; it's the same with man! Then, who is an animal and who is a man? How can the difference be discerned? It is through *dharma* alone. Human beings observe the

---

6 Internal and external purity
7 Virtuous conduct
8 Various states of ultimate perfection

tenets of *dharma*; animals do not. A human being who is without *dharma* can be likened to an animal even if he is without horns and a tail.

112. What is that *dharma*? *Ko naamaso dharmah dhriyate yenase dharmah.* He who has harboured the vast and universal form of this world, that is *dharma*.

113. What is *dharma*? *Bhoot dayaa*, to show compassion towards all creatures is *dharma*. There are other definitions of *dharma*: *yatoabhyudayo nih-shreyas siddhih sa dharmah*[9] – that which leads to the attainment of *abhyudaya* (prosperity in this world) and *nishreyasa* (total cessation of pain and attainment of eternal bliss hereafter), is *dharma*.

114. *Dharma satyaajaayate* – *dharma* is born out of truth. *Dayayaa daanen cha vardhate* – it grows with the help of compassion and charity, *kshamaayaam tishtati* – it dwells in forgiveness and *krodhaan nashyanti* – it is destroyed through anger.

115. *Dhaarati lokaan* – that which holds together the multitude of human beings, that which is of the nature of *dhrit*, that which protects virtuous souls, recognize it as *dharma*. That which leads the world to *abhyudaya*[10] and *moksha*[11], is *dharma*.

---

9 Sage Kanad, founder of the *Vaiseshika* system of philosophy, gives this definition of *dharma*, in his *Vaiseshika Sutras*
10 Spiritual and secular well-being and prosperity
11 Final beatitude

116. The man who does not abide by *dharma* destroys his lifespan. In him failure and disparagement are particularly enhanced. Fortune is ruined and misfortune advanced. His ancestors fall from their place in the higher regions.

Fundamental Definitions

Karma Yoga

117. Whatever is done is indeed *karma*; that which is done to please God without any expectation is *karma yoga*.

Jnana ~ Knowledge

118. Knowledge is seeing Brahma everywhere.

119. *Jnanam Utpadyatey Pumsam Kshayat Papasya Karmanah. Jnana* [true knowledge], comes when sin is destroyed.

120. *Vasudevah Sarvam* – whatever exists is all God – when this knowledge comes, then no sorrow remains. The world then looks like a garden of flowers, of *ananda*. The person then moves about happily in the garden of *ananda*. The screen before his eyes, which makes him see many, is removed and he finds only *ananda*. Everything gets filled with the same *ananda* and everything appears the same.

Bhakti ~ Devotion

121. Well, people talk about *bhakti*. What is this *bhakti*? What are the signs of *bhakti* by which even God melts? *Bhakti* has many signs. Sri Narada said, *Saa Kasmai Param Premarupaa* (absolute love for God is *Premarupaa Bhakti*).

Sa Para-anuraktir-ishvare – to have deep attachment for God is *bhakti*.

Kathaawdisha Anuraagh Bhaktih – to have a liking for stories and *leelas* (divine sport) of God, is called *bhakti*. This was said by *Gargacharya*.

Maharshi Angira has said, *Saa-anuraga Rupa* – due to abundance of *shraddhaa*, to have extraordinary devotion to God is called *bhakti*.

Sri Vyasa Deva has said, *Pujaadishwa-anuraagah Bhaktih* – to have liking for *puja* and other rituals is called *bhakti*.

122. The Vaishnava Acharyas have delienated that *Uttam* (good) *Bhakti* into three types: *Saa Bhakti Saadhanam Bhaav Premaa Cheti Tridhochyate*

123. Whatever feeling of devotion can be grown by concentrating one's senses, that is common *bhakti* and is known as *Sadhan Bhakti*. This awakens the love and devotion which lie dormant in a one's heart; hence

it is called *Sadhan Bhakti*. The *bhakti* which generates *snigdhataa* (i.e. softness or mellowness) in the heart, like the rays of the sun of *prema*, in the form of pure *sattva* is called *Bhava* (ecstatic devotional)*Bhakti*.

124. *Bhava* is the first stage of *prema* (the lasting *bhakti*). When *bhava* grows strong, then it is called *prema*, which is the final result of all effort. *Prema* is the constant *dharma* (duty) of every living creature. Prema is *artha* (the aim of existence – *dharma, artha, kaam, moksha*) – *Chaitanya Shikshamrit*. *Bhakti* consists in being loyally devoted to God.

New Non-Duality

125. There is no *Neti, Neti*[12] philosophy of *Vedanta* here. No *advaita* philosophy either. There is only you and your Beloved! It is by sporting with this God that you will be free of all the sport.

Vishaad[13] ~ True Dispassion

126. When there is affliction, disease, or loss of wife, child, or wealth etc., the righteous individual at once becomes melancholic and there arises in him a desire to dispel his melancholy.

---

12 In Hinduism, and in particular *Jnana Yoga* and *Advaita Vedanta*, 'neti neti' may be a chant or *mantra*, meaning 'not this, not this', or 'neither this, nor that' (*neti* is *sandhi* from *na iti* 'not so') *Neti neti* is a saying found in the *Upanishads*, especially attributed to the *Avadhuta Gita*. *Neti neti* is also an analytical process of conceptualizing something by clearly defining what it is not.
13 Disenchantment – the *Bhagavad Gita* begins with Arjun's *vishaad*

Yoga & Jnana

127. To still the *prana* with the mind is *jnana*; to still the mind through the *prana* is *yoga*.

Aspiring God-Realization

128. Those who perform their spiritual practice with death in view alone are true *sadhakas*[14].

129. God is (ever) ready to reveal Himself to you – the mirror of your heart is lacking in mercury coating. How can you then see the reflection of God therein?

130. If you wish to see God, you will have to eat pure food, be of virtuous conduct, follow the *Sandhya* and *Aahnika* rites[15], obey the commands of God, cultivate the company of holy men and undertake to read and study religious texts, only then will you be able to clean the mirror of your heart for God to reflect in it. These are the duties necessary for those who want Sri Bhagawan Satchitananda[16].
    o Pure and *sattvik* food habits
    o *Yathakaal Upasana* (*Sandhya* and *mantra japa* of favourite deity)
    o *Brahmacharya* (control of sexual instinct, restraint in speech, thought and deed)
    o *Swadhyaya* (undertaking reading of scriptural texts in accordance with your spiritual practice)
    o *Satsanga* (company of devoted saints)

---

14 Spiritual aspirants
15 Daily prayers prescribed in the scriptures
16 Omnipresent, super-conscious and ever-blissful God

Through these, human beings can surely be peaceful. But due to earlier impurities in the body, and eating of prohibited food such as meat, egg, onion etc., it is necessary to go through penitentiary acts as prescribed by the *Shastras*.

131. When the *bhakta*[17] forsakes everything for the sake of obtaining God's *darshan*[18], so much so that he is willing to give up the attachment to his life, then God too cannot stay unmoved, He grants *darshan* and boons!

132. Those who wish to realize God cannot afford to have even the slightest trace of attachment; any attachment will preclude God-realization. Nobody can attain Him without renouncing everything... it is impossible!

133. You will have to awaken this mighty desire in your heart. Resolve today: 'I don't want anything more – wealth, woman, offspring, fame, success – I want nothing. All I want is You!' When you say this and stake all your might, all your life, to this end, you will surely see Him. You will certainly have Him.

134. If you are saying: 'I am chanting *Naam* regularly, why have I not been able to see God?' Listen, this is the answer. You are unable to see Him because you simply don't wish to see Him. The day you are

17 Devotee
18 Direct vision

63

disturbed with an unbearable desire to see Him, that very day you will behold Him.

135. Through *mantra, hatha, laya* and other forms of *yoga,* the human being is able to renounce the defects incurred from *karmas* performed earlier and gain freedom. *Yoga* is the means to overcome these defects.

136. When *this* devotee and God-lover invoked the loving God with great longing, He vouchsafed *darshan* to him in the form of his favourite deity, but that *darshan* was more like a dream and the Lord disappeared as soon as He gave *darshan*. Such vision cannot enable one to understand the true nature of God. There is intense grief or sorrow in it (like that of a lover who is separated from his beloved). To perceive God in a fixed manifestation – a devotee cannot be content with this.

137. The life of loving devotees becomes surcharged with bliss. They gladly and perpetually sport in that ocean of bliss like drops of water. In every direction they experience the existence of Beloved (God). They are unable to perceive anything else (but God).

138. Only when the mind is concentrated on a single object through prayer, *prana* is established in *sahasrara,*[19] and the *bindu*[20] is stilled, should one talk about *jnana*[21].

---

19 thousand-petalled lotus on the crown of the head
20 Lit. Dot, locus of supraconscious awareness
21 transcendental knowledge

The talk of *jnana* from a person of impure mind is insane chatter, delirious rambling and nothing more.

Sadhana, Spiritual Journey & Practice

139. As long as man does not develop love and interest in spiritual practice, the din of the outside world remains.

140. Your *sadhana* begins by getting into a pattern of offering a *pranaam* to Lord saying: 'You are everything' and ends with the practical realization of the fact, 'You are everything'.

141. The aim of *Arya Sadhana* is to annul the ignorance of unity of body and the soul and to establish oneself in an unbroken 'I' who is one without the other.

142. *Upasana* (prayer) is of four types – *Naam* (name), *Rupa* (form), *Leela* (divine sport), and *Dhaam* (abode). Each of these four has unlimited power; each is God Himself. First comes *Naam*, then follows *Rupa*; the third is *Leela* and the fourth is *Dhaam*. If a person can develop single-minded devotion to any of these four, he will be able to cross the ocean of *samsara* with the greatest ease. Each has a bearing on the other. If a person can hold fast to any of them, the others gradually will come by themselves.

143. As a result of the deeds done in previous lives, one comes into this world with specific qualifications. One's *sadhana* depends on one's qualification so acquired. It is in accordance with the path one has followed in previous lives. Hence, one has to select the path for which he is qualified. At the beginning of *sadhana*, one hears of many different paths. As one progresses, all paths meets as one. Whether he is *Shakta* or *Vaishnava*, *Shaiva*, *Soura* or *Ganapatya*[22], whether he is Hindu or Muslim or Christian – all ultimately reach that one path leading to God.

144. Many troubles and obstacles visit the path. They are bound to come – you just keep calling God and make progress! Don't forget *Naam*[23]!

145. Like the flood and ebb tides in the Ganga – there are flood and ebb tides in the spiritual world as well. But don't worry. Once the *kundalini shakti*[24] is awakened, she is bound to steer you back home safely.

146. Just as there is a day and night, one after the other. So it is in the spiritual world as well. There is nothing to worry though; one must continue to practice *sadhana* (spiritual practice) to the best of one's ability.

---

22 Five principal streams of belief in Hinduism; worshippers of the Mother Goddess, Vishnu, Shiva, the Sun and Ganapati, respectively
23 *Tarak Brahma Naam i.e. Hare Krishna Hare Krishna Krishna Krishna Hare Hare, Hare Ram Hare Ram Ram Ram Hare Hare*
24 *Kundalini* is described as a sleeping, dormant potential force in the human organism. Many term it the serpent power because it lies coiled. It is one of the components of an esoteric description of man's 'subtle body', which consists of *naadis*(energy channels), *chakras* (psychic centres), *prana* (subtle energy), and *bindu* (drops of essence).

147. There is no use just reading or hearing about things. It is necessary to carry out *sadhana*. It is impossible to find peace without *sadhana* in any *yuga*.

148. *Sadhana* does not mean becoming a great soul overnight – it's a lifelong battle.

Essence of *Sadhana* ~ Spiritual Practice

149. Let me tell you the gist of all *sadhanas* (spiritual practices) in a nutshell: to hear of His Name and divine attributes with the ears; singing His praise through speech and contemplating on Him with your mind; this is indeed *Mahasadhan* (the supreme spiritual recourse).

150. Chanting of *Naam*, study of scriptural texts, *mauna*[25], are all parts of spiritual practice. If someone undertakes to pray only through *Naam* and reading of religious texts, he will achieve his end only through this. He won't have to open books and study them. When one reads in soft tones thinking that God is listening, the heart and soul is filled with joy.

151. Listen, my dears! Enthrone the commands of God like *aharahah sandhyamupaasit*[26], *aachaarhinam na poonanti vedah*[27], *aahaar shuddhi sattva shuddhih sattva shuddhau dhruvaa smritih*[28] etc. in the seat of God and try to follow them; great good will follow you.

---

25 Vow of silence
26 (O twice-born class!) perform *sandhya* every day
27 Even the *Vedas* cannot purify a person of bad conduct
28 Purification of diet leads to enhancement of the *sattva* quality, which in turns leads to unbroken memory (of God)

152. Believe in the *Shastras* (scriptures). Offer your prayers at appropriate times. Be devoted to your father, mother, Guru and elders. Partake of pure food and conduct yourself virtuously; you will be able to realize that the fountain of infinite happiness lies within your own heart.

153. If you wish to conquer death, stake your life and try to act in accordance with what the venerable elders and preceptors command you. If you do this, you will certainly win the world, you surely will!

154. Practice lying prostrate before the elders and the deity, thrice every day, consume *sattvik* food, observe *brahmacharya*, and endeavour to enhance *sattva guna*[29] through pure thinking.

155. To begin with, listen to the Name and divine sport, thereafter sing *kirtan*, meditation will come of its own. Simultaneously reflect upon the divine history of your favourite deity.

156. In the case of those to whom Guru has designated an *Ishta* (favourite deity), texts concerning the same deity should be heard or contemplated upon.

157. Not only for a *sadhu*, even for all men and women, restraint, moderation in eating, devotion to religion, and belief in God are pertinent.

---

29 Mode of pure intelligence and goodness

3

OMNIPRESENCE – EVERYTHING IS GOD

158. God exists; even today human beings are able to see Him – this is a statement of truth, of extreme veracity, an absolutely great truth.

159. God exists, he reveals Himself – firmly believing in this, and aspiring to obtain *darshan*, keep praying at God's feet.

160. God exists. The ultimate goal of human beings is to have direct *darshan* of God. You must strive with all your heart to achieve this. It is indeed true that it is very difficult to realize God in other *yugas*, but in this hallowed *Kali Yuga*, it is possible to win God through the chanting of *Naam* alone.

161. *samatvam-aaraadhanam-achyutasya: samatva* or adopting an attitude of equanimity, amounts to worshipping Achyuta (Lord Vishnu). Prahlad asked his father, 'Father, how can one have feelings of

friendliness and enmity regarding Him who is the soul of all beings, the Lord, world-pervading, supreme soul Govinda? Lord Vishnu resides in you, in me and everywhere else.'

162. 'You should cover with God everything that you find in this ephemeral world. Enjoy whatever is given to you by Him and do not covet the wealth of others.' From this passage in the *shruti* we learn that all things are to be covered with that Supreme Person, that is, all things are to be viewed as subsisting only in Him. Just as various kinds of earthen pots are nothing but earth, similarly we are to understand that all objects belong to the Supreme cause, God, and one should enjoy only those things which He gives for the maintenance of the body (which one owes to Him), making it a point to view everything as subsisting in the *atman*.

163. The waves are no different from the ocean, in the same way, though men and women, birds and beasts, insects and worms, appear in different forms, there is nothing in this world other than God.

164. There is just one life force behind all beings. One *akasha*[1] has given rise to *vayu*[2], it is just one Lord of all lives who is performing the divine sport, and He has assumed the shape of Sitaram and all of you. Even

1 Ether
2 Air

though the bodies are different, the life force is the same. Just one Being has assumed several forms.

165. *Omkar*, *Atma* and *Brahma* are the names of just one Supreme Being. A desire sprang in Him: 'I shall be many', that is the reason He is performing the divine sport, assuming various forms.

166. The root cause of this world is God's desire – 'I shall be many, I will assume a body'. God alone is performing His *leela* by assuming *naam-rupa* (Name and Form).

167. Assuming varied forms He alone performs *leela*[3]. Spiritual practices and worship is directed towards unfolding this *leela*, the mystery of His divine sport. The differences are perceived because of the *daivi maya* (His deluding potency).

168. The underlying truth is one. God willed – *Bahu syaam prajaayeya* (God resolved to become many). It is He who has taken many forms to enact His divine sport. Creation is His outgoing will. When a person is directed inwards, he takes recourse to the *Shastras* and undertakes spiritual practices in order to realize God. While performing spiritual practices he gains experiences, and then finding the Beloved of his heart in his own heart, he is fully immersed in bliss.

---

3 Divine Sport

169. God alone is performing His Divine Sport adorned in varied attires. Bliss! Man can obtain pure and unalloyed bliss by taking recourse to pure diet, *Naam kirtana* and *Gayatri japa*.

170. 'My Lord has assumed so many guises and He is sporting. Everything is your manifestation, everything is you', contemplate in this manner. This is the highest contemplation. The joy that exists in the contemplation that, 'Everything is your manifestation', is unique, it cannot be found in any other thought or ontemplation. 'Everything is your manifestation, everything is You.'

171. Whatever you are seeing through your eyes – animal, bird, tree, creeper, man, sky, mountain, ocean – each one of them is He. Whatever you are eating is also He. The water you are drinking is He. Wherever you are putting your feet on is also He. Where you are sleeping is His body. He could not take the form of a small human being and stay near you always. Today He has assumed the form of everything, every being, and is keeping you close to His heart. Whatever you see, hear or eat, all these are He. You get submerged in all of them by bowing down to Him.

172. Everything in this world is God. All religious and spiritual practices; services or worships, have for their end, the production of this sentiment.

173. We have now found the essential link with *atma* (soul) – He is the Ear of the ear (the auditory power of the ear), the power of speech of the tongue, the Life of life. He is the dwelling place of sense organs like eyes, ears etc. *Atma* is nothing but the true power of perception.

174. Hari – in the form of earth, I bow to Thee! Rama in the form of water, I salute Thee! Rama in the guise of fire – I bow to Thee! Hari in the form of air – I salute Thee! Hari in the form of void – I salute Thee! Now, hide, eh! Find a nook where you can take cover! Sound, touch, colour, taste, smell – everything is none but You! I bow to You. I bow down to You who have assumed the forms of the different special senses working through the ears, the skin, the eyes, the tongue, the nostrils, the hands the feet, the anus and the genital organ! Aren't you the same who is playing the roles of the deities – Dik, Vayu, Surya, Pracheta, Ashwini Kumars, Agni, Indra, Upendra, Yama and Prajapati: I salute Thee. You are the *materia prima* (*prakriti*); You are the conscious principle of spirit (*purusha*); and I remain saluting you millions and millions of times. You are the essence of the internal sense organ, the intellect (*buddhi*); the sentience (*chitta*) and the ego (*ahamkara*). I bow to Thee. Salutations to You – O, the Infinite, the Indivisible, the Illimitable, the Vast and the Greatest!

Practice in View of God's Omnipresence

175. 'Everything is an extension of God's body'– with this in mind, practice offering *pranaam*[4]. Do not address harsh words to anyone. With a smile on your face, speak sweet words to people.

176. Whatever obstacle you confront, blow it up with the cannon of 'Everything is Your[5] manifestation'! Whatever situation arises, whether favourable or unfavourable, overcome it with the *mantra*: 'Everything is Your manifestation!'

177. Start seeing Me in every object. In all the sounds, hear Me; in all the tastes, taste Me; smell Me in all the smells – I am holding you in my lap, just turn back and see.

178. When one reflects, 'You are everything. There's nothing that's not You. Even in Your forgetfulness, it is You alone', then the mind becomes calm.

179. Once there is a firm belief that disease, sorrow, distress, want, debt, wealth, happiness and peace, that You (God) are all these – the mind will no longer be agitated.

180. If you don't engage your mind in divine sport or form of God, your mind is likely to conjure up the world, become worldly and make a big hue and cry.

---

4 Salutation or prostration
5 God's

Everything is Auspicious

181. To turn your face away from Shiva is to court sorrow. Shiva is *mangal*[6], a mine of auspiciousness! Those men and women who forsake this *mangal*, how can they hope to meet with good fortune?

182. God is the perpetual embodiment of goodness! Whatever He does, it's always for the good, so sing the *Vedas* and *Puranas*.

183. All is good, honour is good, dishonour is good, happiness is good, sorrow is good, a widow is good, a woman with her husband living is good, a son is good, a daughter is good, there is only good and nothing else. God, who is All-Good, has created this universe only of good. Victory to God who is All-Good!

184. The book of your life has already been written. You only turn the pages. Whatever happens will be for your good. In this world there is nothing which is not good.Bhagawan is always *mangalmaya* (all propitious). Whatever He does is all *mangal* – so declare the *Vedas* and the *Puranas*.

185. Know this for sure – whatever God does is auspicious and for our betterment.

186. In every transaction, one must be patient. He is doing only that which is best for us.

6 Auspicious, propitious, that which constitutes spiritual and material good

187. Sri Bhagawan (God) has two feet: *dakshin* and *vaam* – right and left. Happiness, peace and joys are the right foot and disease, grief and distress are the left foot. No matter which foot He extends in front of you, clasp it saying 'Guru', Guru' – this is the remedy to overcome happiness and sorrow.

188. Listen O Mother! The book is already written. Just keep turning the pages. Whatever happens from time to time is auspicious, well-decreed; nothing is inauspicious in the whole world.

189. 'Whatever God does, it is always for the good' – these are the words of our Thakur. In my long life I have experienced the truth of this statement again and again, which is why my throat is never tired of proclaiming it loudly.

190. What God does is for good. This message is the remedy and panacea for all the ills, suffering and sorrow afflicting human beings. He who drinks this medicine gets rid of all three types of ailments – *adhibhautik* (physical, pertaining to the gross body), *adhidaivik* (mental, emotional and *praanic*, pertaining to the subtle body) and *adhyaatmik* (spiritual, pertaining to the astral body). Just as sunlight dispels darkness, or the wind scatters dried leaves, the faith that 'what God does is for good', if held onto unflinchingly, will eliminate all three types of ailments for good!

191. By bestowing disease God seeks our good. A man learns to repeat 'Ram', 'Ram' in disease. He stops making a hullabaloo about this dream-like world.

192. Our God is always benevolent. He extends his benevolence all the time. But human beings, due to their want of proper understanding and thinking about their own selves, hanker after those things which in their little intelligence, appear to be good for them, and moan at their failure to get them. That God, who is directing the universe, lights the way to the attainment of divine bliss by causing seemingly trivial incidents to occur, is a fact which can be tested by any human being. If one remembers this *Maha Mantra* (Our God is always benevolent) in all conditions, Man can enjoy peace wherever he is.

193. It is, however, true that in times of danger one cannot remember this *Maha Mantra*. *Sadhus* have shown the way to remembering it and that is the recital of the *Naam* of Shri Bhagawan at all times. Let sorrow, illness or want come; you must take them all smilingly in your stride.

194. Always keep repeating 'Ram, Ram' and firmly believe that, 'Whatever God does, it is for one's good', then sorrows, distress, disease – none of it will overwhelm you.

Suffering Is Good

195. *Sukhasya Dukhasya na kopidaataa* (happiness or unhappiness is not given by anybody else). Human beings enjoy happiness or undergoe sorrow as a consequence of their *karma*. God does away with *punya* (the merit of good deeds) by giving happiness and He wipes out *paap* (sins) by giving sorrow.

196. Just keep calling out! He knows better than you what is good for you and what is bad. What has been God-given must be reasonable – it has to be! Why fear?

197. Brother, there is nothing in this world like suffering. The more suffering there is, the more does the human being embrace God.

198. Pleasure we crave, though pleasure never comes. For pleasure that is never to be found, we give our precious lives away. But look at pain, pain comes unsolicited. For pain we need not strive or pine. Pain needs no invocation. It comes of itself. Why cannot we hail pain, saying 'Come pain! I am prepared to meet thee'. We do not do so for the simple reason that pain is distressing. Therefore, we long for pleasure that is short lived; whereas pain can bestow everlasting bliss.

199. The Lord says, *maharogo mahashoko mad-anugraha-lakshanam* – great disease and great sorrow are signs of My Grace. The *shrutis* declare loudly and clearly

that even disease is a kind of *tapasya*[7]. Just as *tapasya* results in destruction of sins, disease too destroys sins.

200. How many woes have you gone through? Think of Mother Sita – she suffered despite being the wife of God. Think of Nala and Damayanti. Think of the tale of Srivatsa's distress. Think of the misfortunes of the Pandavas. Think of the pain of Nanda and Yashoda, boon companions of Krishna, of beloved Radha and other consorts. (*There is no such thing as 'why me?'*)

201. A man is poor, has nothing to eat, if he gets food in one part of the day he does not get it in the other. What good does God do in this case? Well, if a man is poor he is not proud; he can understand the sorrow of the poor. People hate a poor man, he cannot be approached. Whomsoever he approaches thinks that he has come to ask for something. Everybody avoids a poor man lest he should want anything. A poor man has no way other than living in solitude. Living in solitude, he gets response from his own near and dear one living in his heart: God! Then he talks with Him, becomes acquainted with Him and lives day and night joyfully with Him. The *sadhus* love the poor very much. They step into the house of a poor man to gratify him and bring him nearer to God. He receives the grace God. God is the wealth of the destitute. He stays away from a man so long as he

7 Austerity

has something to call his own. As soon as all that he had is exhausted, God comes and takes him up in his bosom. This is the eternal way of God.

202. The torment of *samsara* gives a new path to the human being. The majority of people who have taken to the path of God have gone through suffering in this world.

203. Like birth, even the nature of death is predetermined. Devotees who are under the shelter of great saints attain to a higher state even if faced with untimely death.

4

DOSH DARSHAN (Fault-Finding) & *PARA NINDAA* (Criticizing Others)

Essential Oneness in All: Reason for Not Criticizing

204. This is what has been my experience from the long life I have led: a human being is not his own master in performing virtuous or sinful deeds (*paap-punya*). His past *karmas* impel him to helplessly pursue virtuous and sinful deeds. I urge you, therefore, not to harbour an unequal vision and regard people as virtuous or sinners. The sentiment that everything is the divine sport of my *Ishta Deva*[1] will ensure that the mind is not ruffled.

205. Attraction and love for another is actually attraction and love for one's own self – this is actually the attraction towards one's own *atma* (soul).

206. No one is *paraayaa. Par*[2] is *Parameshwar; par* is the venerable *Ishta Deva* for all of us.

---

1 Favourite deity
2 Not kin, not one's own

207. The same being is worshipping and receiving worship, assuming the roles of worshipper and the worshiped Master.

208. Everything is God – no matter whom you insult; you are insulting God. To find fault with someone is to find fault with God.

209. Just as earthenware cooking pots, pitchers and bowls etc. can be fashioned out of clay, in the same way this world is fashioned out of God. There is nothing in this world that isn't God.

210. You have heard this often in the *Shastras*, from the holy men and the mouth of the Guru – your *Ishta Deva* (favourite deity) has assumed multiple forms to perform His *leela* (divine sport). Despite knowing this, how can you criticize or injure others who are none other than your *Ishta Deva*? Tell me O traveller! Tell me, O traitor of the *Ishta*! What can you expect other than suffering? If anyone tries to slap a mountain, will not the hand get injured? If you kick fire, will not the foot burn?

211. Let not the tongue censure anyone or speak ill of anyone, let it not speak harsh words. This is a grave offence, it is impossible to advance spiritually with such things – you surely cannot! God alone performs this divine sport assuming different forms; whomever you reproach; in him you will reproach God.

Not Finding Fault – Way to Self-Perfection

212. Don't see anyone's fault. That alone will make you good. If a person finds faults with others, he attracts those faults to himself and acquires all those faults. So if you really want to be good, don't see other's faults. There is no bigger sin than finding fault with others. One who has committed a wrong, has done it and got its evil effects; but if you go on proclaiming his wrongs and denouncing him, you make your tongue foul and, thereafter, you go on crying. You have been gifted with a pair of eyes so that you may see God in everything and do *pranaam*[3] to all; you have been given a tongue so that you may sing God's *Naam, Rupa* (form), *Leela* (play) and *Guna* (qualities). But if you engage the same eyes and tongue to see and denounce other people's faults, tell me who is there in this world more unfortunate than yourself?

213. O traveller! Do you wish to become a better human being, but you are not able to become one? Are you sad because of this? Would you like to know the reason you aren't becoming better? That's because you haven't learnt to see your own faults. In the same way as you see the faults in others; cleverly start seeing your own faults, then you will become better.

214. Get rid of the defects of your body one by one; be free of every defect. Then the mind won't be directed

---

3 Paying obeisance by joining palms, bowing down or falling flat to the ground

83

outwards; it will enjoy the company of the intimate inner soul and it will obtain supreme bliss and accomplish its purpose.

215. Sri Krishna has declared in the Gita, '*Maam namaskuru* (offer obeisance unto me).' The more you are free from defects, the more particular will you be in chanting *Naam*. Make it a practice to offer *pranaam* while singing *Naam*. You will become perfect; you will definitely become perfect.

216. Whoever has become better in this world has done so by doing away with faults within one's own self.

217. Beware! If you are keen on self-development, swear that you will stop seeing faults in others and start seeing them in yourself alone.

218. Don't see faults in others – always try to see your own fault – you will become a better person soon. It is your faults that keep you from experiencing your own blissful nature.

219. This is our precept: we will not see any fault whatsoever in anyone; if anyone notices fault in us and criticizes us, we will treat it as their kindness. We will think they are reproaching us, and in doing so taking on our sins, hence they are worthy of our respect.

220. As long as there is fault in a man, he can see fault in others; the day he is unable to see fault in others, he can assume God has accepted him – there is no fault in Him. This is the reason everyone must mentally offer *pranaam* to others.

221. Since God has given you two ears, it's better you listen to the divine attributes and sport of God as long as you have the power to listen. Slander of others and futile speech have caused suffering to the ears. Feed them relentlessly by chanting God's Name always, they will attain blessedness, they won't crave to hear any other words – other words will seem like poison.

222. Be kind to me, oh my Dearest, you exist in the garb of one and all. You are ever anxious to purify me, to make me yours, to make me one with you. Please make me understand, make me believe; create faith in me so that I do not pick fault in others. Please mould me in such a way that, remembering that 'you are everything' and believing it with all my mind and heart, I may remain engaged always in singing your praise. Please make me capable of picking my own faults one by one and offering each fault at your feet in *puja* and thus become one with you.

Fault-Finding & the Perils of Criticism

223. Among the offences which bring harm to oneself, there is no sin greater than *para nindaa* (speaking ill of others).

224. It is in the nature of good people to praise, and it is in the nature of the evil people to condemn, therefore one should not be happy or disenchanted listening to them.

225. Listen to me, you exponent of *vaastavika-vaad* (realism)! Do you know how many moments your realism will last? Every trace of your very existence and that of your dependents can be wiped out today. Are you aware of that? Can you imagine it? These things are common occurrence; one often hears of people leaving for an unknown abode in a moment. How real is that?

226. Whoever you think of, that person's stock of virtue, sins, good and evil alike, is automatically contemplated. When you see the face of a sinful one, speak to or think of him, his sins flow to you. One can understand the effect of company through this. By association the mind is immediately polluted.

227. Until such time that his sins aren't dispelled, man cannot renounce the tendency to discriminate, quarrel and so on.

228 If anyone (appearing as your *Ishta Deva*[4]) addresses two words of abuse to you, keep quiet, reflecting that it is for your own good and try to see your own fault. Don't get angry and return the abuse with ten words.

4 Favourite deity

229. No matter how others behave, with a smile on your face, serve them treating it as the blessing of Thakur. Don't see fault in anyone, and see your own failings.

230. Don't look at the faults of others. Don't criticize others. Practice offering *pranaam* saying, 'Namaste bahurupaaya[5]'.

231. At every step, in proving the other person guilty and yourself innocent, you are experiencing self-delight; but that is not delight, it is suicide.

232. The distinguishing feature of a mean person is to publicise the faults of others. Such a person tries to garner people's approval in favour of 'I am a good man'; but censure is such a terrible thing that it heaps sin not only on the one who carps at others but also the one who listens to such slander.

233. To slander or criticise others and to destroy oneself is one and the same thing. You have to accept the sins of the person whom you have criticised. Actually it is one's own *Ishta Devata* (favourite deity) who arranges everything, assuming different forms. Through slander, one is deprived of that supreme truth and have to wander in sorrow, lifetime after lifetime.

---

5 Salutations to Him, who appears in multiple forms

234. There is no other way to win over enemies disguised as friends, than abandoning co-operation. There is no other way than to practice non-cooperation.

Non-Enmity

235. Even inadvertently, do not entertain a thought in your mind that anyone is your enemy. 'My *Ishta Devata* (favourite deity) alone has assumed myriad forms and is bringing an end to auspicious and inauspicious *karmas*' – this should be your belief.

5

COMMON *DHARMA*

Satya ~ Truth

236. Speak the truth. *Satya* (Truth) itself is God. He, who takes refuge in truth, reaches his desired goal speedily.

237. Always speak the truth. Whether in speech, thought or deed, do not resort to falsehood of any kind.

238. Beware of the tongue; speak less and let not your tongue utter false or useless things.

239. *Satya* is *Bhagawan* (God). He who takes refuge in truth realizes God. There is no sin greater than falsehood.

240. Whatever you resolve, or speak: try to defend and stick to it. When you succeed in this, you will realize your intentions – whatever you think of will come true! There will be no futile endeavours.

241. Truth is forever the truth even as *agni*[1] is always *agni*.

Ahimsa ~ Non-violence

242. There is no *dharma* in the world greater than non-violence and there is no greater *adharma* than violence.

243. Renounce *himsa* (violence). Nobody will be able to be inimical towards you.

244. A blanket is made out of wool; despite the fact that it is a pure material, the *vaishnavas*[2] did not use it because it was made by troubling a creature and cutting its hair.

Common *Dharma*

245. *Ahimsa, Satya, Astyeya, Shauch* and *Indriya Nigraha*, are common *dharma* for everyone. (Their definitions follow.)

246. *Ahimsa* means not to inflict violence upon any living creature in word, thought or deed. The principle of *ahimsa* is well-known. The *Bhagavad Gita* stresses *ahimsa* time and again. The Buddha, Mahavir, Christ, were all votaries of *ahimsa*. Mahatama Gandhi proved its successful application even in the political field. One should refrain from committing physical violence

---

1 Fire
2 Follower of *Vaishnavism*, a tradition of Hinduism, distinguished from other schools by its worship of Vishnu or his associated *avatars*, (principally Rama and Krishna), as the original and Supreme God

of course, but equally important is not to do ill to others, not to be jealous of others, not to entertain feelings of enmity, not to abuse or denigrate. This spirit of *ahimsa* can be developed in all people, irrespective of their caste or position in life, by the rich and poor alike.

247. *Satya* (Truth), is the common *dharma* of all the four *varnas*. Non-violence and Truth are the two legs on which *dharma* stands. In fact ,Truth is God and God is Truth. Actually it is Truth from which all other virtues flow. Truth is the very basis of all religions, all morality, and all norms of civic intercourse. And what is Truth for the *Brahmin* is also the Truth for the *Kshatriya* or the *Vaishya* or the *Shudra*. Truth does not make any distinctions of caste. But Truth should be *kalayaankar*, i.e. productive of good result. If it produces bad results, then Truth comes down from its pedestal.

248. *Asteya* means not to steal. Theft does not consist only of the removal of somebody else's property. If one covets somebody else's property, he commits mental theft. Smuggling, black marketing, adulteration, all are different forms of theft. Theft can be done in the field of ideas also. *Asteya* is equally applicable to all castes and creeds.

249. *Indriya-Nigraha* means controlling one's senses. If one succeeds in turning the *Bahirmukhi Indriyas*[3] to

---

3 Outer-directed sense-organs

Antramukhi[4], gradually the eyes will shut themselves to outward things and see the *Jyoti* (divine light) inside, the ears will not hear external music but will hear the *Naad* (divine sound), an extraordinary sense of perception and smell will come and the person will feel the taste of *amrita*[5]. That is the final achievement of *Indriya-Nigraha*.

250. *Shaucha*, i.e. purity or cleanliness, is the common *dharma* of all. This is not confined to the outer body and the environment but to the mind also. Physical purity is achieved with the help of water or earth and also by *ahaar shuddhi*, i.e. eating *sattvik* food, and mental purity by observing *maitri, karuna, mudita* and *upeksha*[6]. This mental *shaucha* comes from non-attachment. If one is not unattached, he will run after results without bothering about the means and that, in its turn, will lead him to avarice, anger and lust – the three gateways to hell, as the *Bhagavad Gita* says.

Control of the Senses

251. A person can gain deliverance by controlling his senses. *Dama* denotes the control of senses which leads one to work. These are all outward senses.

---

4 Inner-directed
5 Nectar of immortality
6 In relationships, the mind is purified by friendliness towards those who are happy, compassion for those who are suffering, goodwill towards those who are virtuous, and indifference/neutrality towards those we perceive as wicked/evil (*maitri karuna mudita upekshanam sukha duhka punya apunya vishayanam bhavanatah chitta prasadanam.* ~ *Patanjali Yoga Sutras* 1:33)

Heart, mind, intellect, and ego – these are all internal senses. Their control is called *shama*. Control does not mean the killing of the senses. Control means to bring them under one's own power. This is *dharma*. Your hand is endowed with outward senses. So the hand always wants to pick up external things. It loves to take such things. That brings in other temptations. So the hand has to be drawn inside. To do this, one should keep both hands touching one's chest while doing *japa*. This is an infallible way of controlling one of the outgoing senses.

252. The best way of doing *tapasya* is to fast. By fasting one can quickly control one's senses. Rich and delicious food makes the senses strong and wayward. Hence it is very necessary for a *sadhak* to eat only *sattvik* food. By having *sattvik* food, one's heart and mind are cleansed. Pure *sattvik* food consists of rice, *moong* or *matar dal*, wheat, barley, *ghee*, milk, butter, green banana, various fruits, roots, various vegetables (except onions, garlic, carrots and turnips), almonds, sugar-cane, molasses, coconuts, pomegranates, grapes, etc. There is no dearth of eatables which can be classified as *sattvik*. So one need not run after *rajasik* or *tamasik* food.

253. Among the senses, the most powerful are the tongue and sex-organ. The tongue has three actions – to taste, to talk and to consume food. The sex-organ has two

functions – to procreate and to touch. If one can control these two senses, the others will get automatically controlled.

254. *Bramcharya* is a fine form of *tapasya*. Fasting, *mauna* (vow of silence), austerity, eating only one meal a day – these are all conductive to *tapasya*.

255. *Tapasya* is of three types – *tapasya* by body, *tapasya* by speech and *tapasya* by mind. To have devotion to God, Brahmins and the Guru, and to worship them, is called bodily *tapasya*. *Tapasya* by speech consists of talking sweetly and modestly, talking reverentially to elders and superiors and as equals to those who are younger or inferior, not to lend one's ears to criticisms and not to criticize others and chant *Naam*. Mental *tapasya* is to cultivate the quality of non-violence, truth, cleanliness, contentment, study of scriptures, etc.

256. The best way to purify one's mind is to do work without any attachment. Unattached work is of three types: i. for pleasing *Bhagawan*; ii. work given by *Bhagawan*; iii. work to carry out the orders of *Bhagawan*.

Work to please *Bhagawan* consists of doing *puja* and *paath*, collecting flowers and preparing garlands, cleaning the place of worship, and offering flowers, fruits, water etc. to *Bhagawan*.

Work given by *Bhagawan* consists of doing *Sandhya-Upasana* three times a day.

One should always think that whatever one is doing the whole day is for the fulfillment of His desires. One must not have the ego that one is doing something or is causing it to be done. 'God is everything and everything is being performed according to His desires. I am only the instrument; it is God who is getting everything done.' Work done in this way is work sent by God and carried out under His orders.

Shraddha ~ True Faith

257. *Shraddha* or faith, is the life of all *sadhanas* (spiritual practices). Where there is no faith, there is nothing.

258. To firmly believe in the words and injunctions of the Guru and *Vedanta*, this is the definition of faith.

259. He who pledges firmly: 'I will walk the path shown by the Guru with an intellect rooted in belief in God's existence and thus accomplish everything,' and follows Guru's instructions unswervingly, such a one is said to be endowed with faith. It is *shradhha* (faith), which confers immortality upon man.

260. What is devotion and spiritual practice? Guru has asked you to chant *Naam*; 'I will follow his command whether I get any experience or not.' By singing *Naam*

with firm faith, *sattvik* sentiments manifest with time.

261. *Shraddha* (faith) is the proposed end of all *siddhis*[7], it is the cause of true knowledge; true knowledge and *shraddha* are indistinguishable. Therefore, after realizing this, disciples who have belief in Guru and the *Mantra*, certainly achieve *Mantra Chaitanya* (spiritualization of their *mantra*), irrespective of the nature of their Guru.

262. Those who are so immersed in evil deeds that they don't care about public censure, fear or insult, or for that matter anything in this world, these have an appropriate turn of the mind; if their consciousness can somehow be directed to God, it can speedily get fixed on God simply because they have a one-pointed mind.

Karma & Nishkaam Karma

263. The *Shastras* say you will have to undergo *prarabddha*[8] or those *karmas*, which constitute this body. Fresh *karmas* won't develop if these *karmas* are exhausted in a lifetime.

264. There is one Being, one relation, who is forever protecting you. He is drawing you closer to His lap. Never forget this. Whatever work you do, treat it as His work and keep doing it. *He* will take the onus.

---

7 One of the eight mystic *yogic* perfections
8 Past *karmas* which have neared fruition

265. *Nishkaam Karma*[9] is divided into three categories:
   i. Performing religious and secular duties in accordance with the command of God.
   ii. Serving God.
   iii. To be free from a sense of doership and thinking that 'I am doing nothing, everything is inspired by God'. Acting in this manner, one is freed of *samsara*.

266. Mother! How much *karma* does a man bring into this world? All that stock will have to be destroyed. It is better to deplete it while singing *Naam*.

267. By acquiring learning and by *Nishkaam Karma*, you set an example to the world. There is no real *jnana* (knowledge) in the books. *Jnana* is the fulfillment of *sadhana;* it is the life force of *tapasya*. If you go on repeating the *Shastras* like an animal or a bird, you will not be able to acquire real *jnana* even after a hundred births. Pray and worship and enlightenment will come to you. Go on doing *sadhana;* the whole power of the Creator of this Universe will come and embrace you.

Tapasya ~ Austerity

268. *Tapasya* results in enhancement of the *sattva* quality, enhancement of the *sattva* quality results in steadiness of mind. Through a steady mind, one can realize the Self. Self-realization is the ultimate aim of human life.

---

9 Working without expectation and surrendering the fruits of one's action to God

269. There are several meanings of the word *tapasya*. *Tapah dvandva sahanam* – *tapasya* is enduring of polar opposites like heat and cold, hunger and thirst, and observance of *vaak mauna* (refraining from speech), *kaashta mauna* (refraining from speech including communication through sign language), *kriccha-chandrayana vrata*[10] etc. Some say *tapasya* is observance of *vratas* or regimes aimed at soothing the mind.

270. The knowledge related to Brahma is known as *tapasya*. Some say the undertaking of fast on *ekadashi* etc. is *tapasya*. The *shrutis* declare *taponaanshanaatparah*. There is no *tapasya* greater than *anashana* (fasting). Some even name *swadhyaaya* as *tapasya*, *samanaska-indriyaanaam-ekaagrakaranam tapah* – *tapasya* is the name given to the effort of concentrating all the sense organs along with the mind on a single object.

271. *Tapasya* bestows on man genuine human nature; it is because man does not snap out of the intoxication of the body that he is unable to reach the origin of joy. It is through *tapasya* that the inebriation of body-consciousness is removed.

272. Those who undertake *tapasya* in order to realize God; those who acquire the knowledge of *pranava*[11], the

---

10 Beginning with fast on the new moon day and having one morsel of food the next day and increasing one by one, morsels of food every day thereafter. Then from the full moon day onwards, again decreasing one by one morsel of food every day and a total fast at the new moon.
11 The mystic sound *Aum/Om*

root cause of this world, through *tapasya*; they are truly blessed.

273. What is the remedy? *Tapasya*, adoption of His *Naam*, hymns, prayers – these are the things. It is strange, human beings have acquired God but due to the lack of *tapasya*, they have to put up with loud lament despite having God.

274. Whatever may be the wealth and prosperity enjoyed by a human being; it is the product of *purva tapasya*, (worship and austerities undertaken earlier). A host of *devas* and sages attained eminence through *tapasya*. Those who are desirous of self-development must consider *tapasya* as their necessary duty.

275. There is no point in getting excited. Everyone has to put in spiritual effort over a long period of time. It is not possible for anyone to perform *sadhana* and become great overnight.

Tyaga ~ Renunciation

276. Renunciation! Renunciation! Well, there can be no sense-gratification once you have renounced.

277. The company of people, honour and fame, are as disastrous as poison for *sadhus*. The foolish *sadhu* who cannot renounce the company of men, has to come to a very sad state indeed.

278. The magnet is bound to attract; ghee is bound to melt; which is why it is essential for *sadhus* to be on guard. If they are not cautious, 'Ram Ram Ram Sitaram', they are bound to be tarnished.

279. Listen, my dear! The devotee does not desire any *dharma, artha, kaam moksha*[12]; all he desires is service unto God. Devotional service alone is his object.

280. Happiness and joy cannot be had until God is found. Renouncing everything, forsaking all objects and saying, 'I seek only God', life will have to be dedicated to God alone.

281. Renounce everything; he who does not renounce cannot gain peace.

282. Judging from your dress, trimmings, and cigarette case, I can clearly see you have no desire to be liberated. He whose head burns with fire, can he be interested in clothes and appearances or worldly life? He who has received the funeral offerings of Ganga water, can he be interested in marrying a sixteen-year-old maiden?

283. All the objects of this world have only sorrow to offer. The extent to which an individual moves away from

---

12 *Dharma* or righteousness; *Artha* or wealth; *Kama* or pleasure of the senses; and *Moksha* or freedom through communion with God/the Infinite. These four attainments of life are collectively known as *Purushartha*.

worldly pleasures is the extent to which he keeps himself aloof from experiencing sorrow. He moves far away (from sorrow).

How to Become Desireless & Dispassionate?

284. If you can't become desireless with effort – fill your heart and mind with *Naam*, there will be no place left for any desire.

285. Continue to endure everything while repeating 'Ram, Ram'– pray for freedom from worldly desires. When it's time for God's grace, wipe away the collyrium of desires, sever the bondage of attachment and renounce *samsara* (worldly existence) dancing with pleasure.

286. Even a mountain of your wealth will not liberate you from this mortal world. Money will only bring misfortune; stay aloof from it.

287. Both effort and detachment are required. Without detachment it is not possible for anyone to continue his spiritual efforts.

Seva ~ Service & Acts of Welfare

288. It is service that takes one to higher regions. Service destroys the sense of 'me' and 'mine', and ending body-consciousness, enables one to realize oneself. It is service that leads one to direct vision of God.

289. Service alone! Service! Service in the material way! Service mentally! The servant does not even realize when and how he became free from the bondage of *samsara*.

Paropakara ~ Service to Others

290. Having been born into this world and acquired the transient human body, one must forever try to engage oneself in serving others to the extent possible. *Paropakara* (welfare of the others), is the supreme *dharma*. The enlightened ones consider their lives fruitful simply by serving mankind.

Just *Seva* ~ Service isn't Enough

291. *Seva*[13] without *upasana*[14] cannot purify the *chitta*[15]. It cannot gain root in firm ground because after performing service for a few days, the *chitta* falls down to its lower state.

292. So long as a person nurses the desire in his heart that he can perform some good work, his work is never properly done. When the heart is clean of all forms of desires and craving for results, only then God gets hold of his body and mind and engages Himself for the good of the world, with him as the instrument. Then whatever work comes to hand, its progress is unchecked and its result assured.

---

13 Devotional or secular service
14 Devotional or spiritual practice
15 Mind-stuff

293. Just *seva* (service) won't do, you will have to regularly do *japa* of 26,600 bead counts. It doesn't matter whether you are a householder or a renunciate; those who have done this, have gained experiences and supreme joy, while those who engaged themselves in *seva* (service) alone, have dropped *seva* after a few days and fallen. It is because of this, many renunciates have fallen from the path.

294. Even while engaged in welfare activities and service, there is the need to do *japa-dhyana* etc. The purpose of service is to realize God, therefore continue welfare work but don't give up *Naam* and contemplation of God's divine sport.

Compassion

295. Among the various paths available for assimilation of *dharma* (virtue), the path of compassion is the most excellent one. It is the compassionate one who is designated a *sadhu* and attains immortality.

Daan ~ Charity

296. *Daan* (charity) brings religious merit to the *daataa* (donor), not the *grahitaa* (recipient).

Grace

297. When one feels naturally drawn to, shows great respect for, listens to, or contemplates on the *Bhagavad Katha*[16], one must take it that grace of *Satguru* has descended.

---

16 Devotional lore

298. *Shuddha-ahara, sadachara, Yathakaal upasana* – pure food, virtuous conduct, and worship at prescribed hours, these three can rain His grace. The grace comes from above, invariably.

Contentment

299. Worldly sorrows cannot reach anywhere near those whose minds have been calmed by drinking the nectar of divine bliss. They constantly dwell in *ananda* (bliss). Sorrow, hardship, suffering and disease run away from them.

Character

300. It is due to the strength of his character that a man is adored like a God or despised like a devil. There is no virtue that can overwhelm one's innate character.

301. A man of sterling character, even if residing in a little hut and filling his stomach with alms obtained from door to door, is still adored by even the gods.

302. Whether it's a man or a woman, character is a priceless wealth for everyone. This wealth once lost cannot be regained. All men and women must preserve this wealth with utmost care.

303. In the short run, prosperity may be achieved through unrighteous means (aversion to *dharma*); then one begins to see good in it. Thereafter, victory is obtained over enemies, shortly after, everything is destroyed.

Shaucha ~ Purity

304. Water is the source of life, from water life is inspired, therefore the length of time you spend in water for a bath etc., makes your body healthy and the energy of *prana* is enhanced. That is why the first instruction of the *Aryan rishis* was to take a bath in the morning.

305. Rising early in the morning and performing daily ablutions, one must bathe. Through bathing in the morning, both the body and mind are endowed with *sattvik bhava*[17]. The *Shastras* declare that the morning bath rids one of infinite sins.

---

17 Sentiments of purity and goodness

.

6

NATURE OF THE *GURU*

306. Guru can never be *asat* (untrue). Bhagawan Sri Ram used the epithet *Sat Guru*, to describe the preceptor who confers liberation from worldly existence.

307. Even a great fool who sings the praise of Guru must be considered a scholarly *pundit*.

308. Without taking refuge with the Guru it is impossible to take even a single step forward in worldly or spiritual life. Guru is the sole refuge of all.

309. Those who implicitly believe in devotion to Guru and Guru's word, they are able to gain supreme bliss – there is no room for doubt in this. *Guru kripa hi kevalam* (Guru's Grace alone is absolute)!

310. Human beings have three *Maha-Gurus*: one's mother, one's father and one's spiritual preceptor. One must show great devotion to them. Their welfare and

desires should be attended to. Whether little or more, whoever gives you spiritual knowledge, he should be recognized as a Guru.

311. Assuming a human body God has descended on earth to rescue sinners – all distress vanishes by adopting a Guru. Mysterious are the sweet feet of the Guru! O tongue, sing the name of Guru! O mind, contemplate on Guru's abode! O head, bow down regularly in every watch of the day before the soft lotus feet of the Guru.

312. Crazy mind! Learn this wisdom: the heart blooms as you say 'Guru Guru Guru'. See the form of the Guru with the eyes. Listen to Guru's teachings with the ears. Always meditate with your mind focused in the thousand-petalled lotus in the forehead and make the mystery of this world as lucid as the cow's hoof.

313. Do not forget Guru is the embodiment of Brahma, Vishnu and Maheshwara. He assumes the human body in order to grace and consecrate human beings.

314. First concern yourself with obtaining Guru; once you take refuge with Guru, all your woes and worries will cease, he will usher you on the path of God. You won't have to think of anything else. You will be free from all worries.

315. A father gifts the body; Guru gifts knowledge; therefore in the sorrowful ocean of worldly existence, there is none greater than Guru.

316. *Satguru*[1] and God are not different; God Himself appears in the form of Guru.

317. What do you mean by distinguishing between Guru and Shiva? Gurudeva is Shiva personified – He is omniscient. He knows everything! The dirty mirror of your heart reveals the sullied image of Gurudeva, but it is not real.

318. Gurudeva is the favourite deity – by contemplating His divine sport the mind effortlessly melts away and steadies. Where and how did you gain *darshan* of Gurudeva? How did he accept you as a disciple? Where did you wander about with Gurudeva? Write down all the special events related to Gurudeva in a notebook and contemplate on it. By contemplating on the divine sport of Gurudeva, the mind will quickly melt away. Try it.

Guru Mantra

319. Try to purify the ground first by repetition of 'Guru', 'Guru'. Once the soil is ready, you will get the seed in fitness of time, and with the receipt of Guru's Grace, you won't have to worry about anything.

---

1 Enlightened Master

320. By being initiated into a *mantra*, the power of the Guru is gained. The *siddha mantra* handed down through spiritual succession takes the spiritual aspirant into inner world extremely fast. The purpose of getting initiation into a *mantra* is to get Guru's Grace. Guru is none other than God. He imparts His own Self through the investment of *mantra*; it is to install Guru in one's heart and happily cross over the ocean of worldly existence that the refuge with the Guru is sought.

321. Sri Gurudeva puts God inside us in the form of *mantra* whispered into the ears.

322. The *mantra* 'Guru' is the supreme lord among all the *mantras* in this world. Without taking recourse to it nobody can advance in the spiritual world.

323. 'Guru', 'Guru', 'Guru', the devotees should do the *japa* of 'Guru', 'Guru', 'Guru' all the time, while standing or sitting, in the day and night. Whoever takes shelter with a Guru, for him the vast ocean of worldly existence becomes small and easy to cross as cow's hoof. Just keep doing the *japa* of 'Guru', 'Guru', 'Guru'.

324. By mere utterance of the sub-syllable 'ga' one is absolved of the heinous sin of Brahmahatya[2], the utterance of 'u' indemnifies the individual from sins committed

---

2 *Brahmahatya*: killing of a *Brahmin*

throughout the life. The remaining three sub-syllables of the magic word 'Guru' viz. the 'ra', the 'u' and the 'hu': once uttered, destroy the cumulative effect of all the sins committed in the past ten million births! By chanting the mantra 'Guru' Lord Shiva absolved Himself from the sin of *Brahmahatya*[3], Parashuram from the transgression of *Matruhatya*[4] and foremost of the gods Indra from the sin of Brahmahimsa.[5]

Guru Protocol

325. A capable disciple swiftly gains perfection if he strives to undertake spiritual practices treating Guru as Lord Shiva incarnate. Tailang Swami[6] often said, '*Guru mile laakhon laakh, shishya na mile ek* (There's no dearth of Gurus, you'll get lakhs of them, but it's hard to find even a single *shishya* [disciple]). Unless one becomes a *satshishya* (true disciple), one cannot hope to gain the grace of a *satguru* (true Guru). As is the disciple, so will the teacher be. Each gets his own match.

326. 'I will act in whichever way my Guru, with whom I have taken refuge, commands me' – this is the duty of a disciple. To conduct oneself according to one's own will is foolishness.

---

3 Killing of a *Brahmin*
4 *Matruhatya*: killing of mother
5 *Brahmahimsa* : violence to those who have attained the state of *Brahma*
6 Shri Tailang Swami was a great *Kriya yogi* and one of the few yogis whose remarkable life, filled with miraculous stories, was historically documented and verified. The name Tailang was mainly used in Varanasi and is reminiscent of Telugu, his mother tongue.

327. After *diksha*, your body is in the possession of God, embodied as Sri Guru. 'I' is turned into 'this servant', 'mine' is turned into 'of this servant' – this is the way to conduct your self.

328. Meditating on Guru-*paduka* (wooden sandals worn by Guru) or on Guru Himself and performing Guru-*puja* (worship of the Guru), with the mind as its sole offering – this should be done at the *sahasrara* (top of the head). External Guru-*puja* or worship of Guru-*paduka* and prayers chanting of *Stava/ Kavacha* (*mantras* to ensure safety and well-being), are various forms of service to Guru. Continuous repeating of *mantra-japa* or by writing the same on the two-petalled lotus (between the eyebrows), and going round the Guru, constitute true service to Guru. Meditating on the *kundalini* at the *muladhara*[7], performance of mental worship, reading/ chanting of prayers and *Kavachas* and meditating that He (the Guru), is permeating through one's entire body – all these constitute His worship. Finally, the *parameshthi* Guru-*puja* (ie. the ultimate form of Guru-worship), is nothing but the uniting of the awakened *kundalini* at *muladhara* with Supreme Shiva dwelling in the form of a *bindu* (pointed light source), at the *sahasrara* (top of the head) after penetrating the six *Chakras*[8].

---

7 Primordial spiritual energy stored at the root of the spine in the form of a coil

8 The six wheels of different levels and forms of spiritual energies located from the bottom of the spine to the top of the head

329. What can a disciple offer to God in the form of Guru who has occupied him completely, both within and externally? He then does not have anything of his own to give because everything belongs to Sri Guru. The best kind of *dakshina* to offer the Guru is to do *sadhan* and *bhajan* according to his instructions. The only *dakshina* which the Guru desires is that his disciple, by dint of his *sadhana*, may be self-fulfilled and may gain immortality. The greatest *dakshina* of a Guru is the gaining of *paramananda* by the disciple.

Guru, *Mantra*, *Ishta*

330. There are two manifestations of God – *saguna* and *nirguna* (God with form, name and attributes and God without these three). As long as a human being has body awareness, there is the feeling that 'I am the body'. He labours in ignorance and forgetfulness of true self. Till then he is entitled only to *saguna* worship.

331. He is the *Ishta Devata* (favourite deity), He comes in the form of Guru; He resides in the form of *mantra*.

332. Without duly recognizing the oneness of Guru, *mantra* and *Ishta*, it is not possible to achieve *mantra siddhi*. Guru is both *mantra* and *Ishta Devata* (favourite deity).

333. Taking Guru to be a human being, treating *mantra* as mere collocation of words, and to seeing the stone in an idol, are all offences leading one to hell.

334. You were born, you were educated, and you went through *samsara*, in all this you are merely a body! One day Gurudeva came into your life and accepted you, you became a disciple. From the time compassionate Gurudeva absorbed you, the body became Gurudeva's; now the body is not your's. It belongs to Gurudeva.

335. How hard does a human being toil to get rid of sorrow? If only a person could do *japa* of the Guru-given *mantra* until it is consummated and realized! That would not only rid him of sorrows but also help him attain divinity.

336. Unless one starts to eat a pure diet, the power to sit still will not arise. You won't be able to do it even in ten long years. If you are keen on realizing God, you'll have to adopt a regime of pure diet.

Diksha ~ Initiation

337. *Diksha* is mandatory for everyone. One needs to receive *diksha* and perform spiritual practices to achieve the state when one can perceive the truth.

338. At the time of Guru conferring *mantra* on the disciple, Lord Shiva manifests in the Guru's body, which is why even if the *mantra* is not spiritually instinct with life, it is activated through *japa, homa* and *purascharan*[9] rites according to the scriptures and

grants *siddhis*. Whatever the desire borne by the aspirant, it is fulfilled when *mantra siddhi* is achieved.

339. Right at the time of initiation, when the Guru gives the **mantra**, he says, *Uttishtha*[10] *vatsa, muktosi*. He says to the disciple who is prostrated himself in all humility, '*O child*, rise. You are free.' The disciple is liberated as soon as he is initiated with a *mantra*. All spiritual activities such as meditation and chanting are only meant to inculcate the feeling that 'I am free!'

Which Form to Meditate On?

340. Whichever form appears while you are meditating, contemplate on that form; there is no need to forcibly conjure images.

Siddhis ~ Spiritual Powers

341. When one's mind becomes steady by keeping company with *sadhus*, by studying the *Vedas* and other religious books, by doing work according to the instructions of the *Shastras*, by the grace of God – he then realizes that he is not shelter-less, he has One with whom he can take shelter. Thereafter, he is not disturbed by pleasure or pain, peace or want of it,

---

9 *Purascharana* means 'prefatory rite'. Typically this is the chanting of a certain number of *mantras* before beginning a fire ceremony. It can also loosely mean a *sankalpa* or resolution to chant a certain *mantra* a certain number of times for a certain number of days (eg. *Om Namah Shivaya*, 108 times for 100 days, so that one would have done more than 100000 repeatitions of the *mantra*)

10 Another context of *Utishtha* is *Uthishta jagrata prapyava – ran nibodhat*, which means, 'Arise, awake, and stop not till the goal is reached'

penury or prosperity, joy or sorrow. He realizes clearly that whatever is happening is for his *mangal* (good). He then constantly stays with *Naam*, and, like a spectator in a film show, watches and enjoys the play of *prakriti* and its endless wonders.

342. *Siddhi* (spiritual powers) is an indication of the fact that one is making progress in spiritual practice. When one performs *sadhana* (spiritual practices), *siddhi* is certain. One must be indifferent to *siddhi* and perform spiritual practices to the best of one's abilities until the main goal is reached. You will surely realize your *Ishta* (favourite deity). You surely will!

343. *Japa, dhyana* and *tapasya* are His forerunners, He sends them ahead to purify the heart of the devotee – human beings do not really do anything. There's only the descent of God.

344. The experience of *Jyoti, Naad*[11] and such other encounters, are not futile imaginings. It takes years to earn a professional degree or post-graduation and be capable of earning money (spiritual experiences likewise don't happen overnight). If a genuine seeker, after liberation, undergoes atonement according to the scriptures and performs spiritual practices as directed by Sri Gurudeva for three months, he is bound to experience the truth of these things, and be blessed with personal realization.

11 Divine effulgence and sound

345. Though the goal is realization of your favourite deity, all the *siddhis* (extraordinary powers) concommitant with it are bestowed, even if you don't wish for them.

346. Through ascetic practice *sattva guna* is acquired, the unattainable is attained; every wish is amply satisfied.

347. Through the grace of Guru the devoted disciples succeed in gaining *siddhis* swiftly.

348. Just as it is meaningless for a beggar to declare 'I don't want a lakh of rupees' because anyway a lakh of rupees is not lying on the street to be picked up, it is meaningless for a person lacking faith in the word of the Guru, and incompetent in renouncing worldly pleasures, to say 'I don't want *siddhis*'.

349. He who pretends to be Shiva and impersonates Him even before actually attaining Shivahood, will have to suffer the burning pain of poison and the striking of the snake.

350. Sometimes fear of death can also loom large, but at that time one must perform spiritual practices with greater determination.

351. Do not desire to acquire *vibhutis*[12], let no thought of gaining honour from people come to your mind. If it does, banish it immediately.

---

12 In the Vibhuti Pada of the *Yoga Sutras,* many different *vibhutis* (paranormal powers) are mentioned

352. *Mantra siddhi* is impossible without firm faith in Gurudeva. Whether the Guru is a fool or a scholar, given to virtuous conduct or evil ways, He is still a *devata* (God). He is the only recourse.

353. The *sadhaka* need no longer meditate on *Omkar* or contemplate after *Naad* comes. Yes, one need only hold onto *Naad*; nothing else is necessary. There is no scope here for the play of imagery or blind faith. The self-effulgent *Naad* plays on without a stop. The *dhyana* of *Naad* alone will open all portals of knowledge. God will hold him fast on His breast.

354. If a *sadhu* merely dresses up in ochre robe and cheats people, it amounts to deceitful behaviour. Efforts aimed at conquering one's own mind can never be deceptive.

Omkar

355. *Om* is My Name and My Potency.

356. By the grace of Sri Guru, when the *sadhaka* becomes one with the *paramatma pranava* by seeing his body merged with his own *atma* in the form of resplendent *pranava*, nothing else remains. He loses consciousness of all company and becomes desireless. He is then at peace with himself. There is no second – so whose company will he seek and what can he hanker for?

He finds that the *omkar*-vibration is the cause of everything, *adhi-daivik*, *adhi-bhauthik* and *adhyatmik* and becomes immersed in *Omkar-Naad* and thus attains liberation. So long as his body remains, his mind plays with *Naad* and *Jyoti*. Though he is seen with a body, he actually exists only in the *Naad* and so becomes like the *akasha* (sky).

357. The seed of all the *Vedas* is the triune of A, U and M –*AUM*, also known as *pranava*. The seed of *aum* is *Hari Naam*. As one chants *Hari Naam*, *Naad* (divine sound) manifests.

358. *Omkar* is the core principle. It is only *Omkar* that pervades this world. And all worship is actually worship of *Omkar*.

359. The Banyan seed is such a small thing, but a huge tree is hidden inside it. It cannot be discerned from external appearances. In the same manner, this whole world has sprung solely from *Omkar*.

360. Once the human being is able to realize the true nature of God within him, he gains the authority of *pranava*[13]. If a person considers that he is eligible for *pranava* before that, and starts *pranava japa*, six foes[14] assail him. He is bound to suffer at their hands.

---

13 The mystic sound *Aum*
14 *Shadripu*, or the six foes/defects of the embodied soul: attachment, pride, anger, envy, passion and greed

361. In every man it is the same *omkar* which causes the performance or sum of all *karmas*. It is working in accordance with each one's *karma rashi*.

362. In order to make the *sadhaka* directly perceive the truth that He is both *nirguna* (without attributes) and *saguna* (with attributes), He is the *atma* and *avatara*, that He is all-in-One, God takes away *Ram Naam* from him and gives him *Omkar* in its place. If he can but hold on to this *Omkar* in the form of *Naad*, then nothing further remains for him to know or do.

363. The disease is to see many. The *sadhaka* should first try to realise that, by the vibration of the *prana*, the *shakti* of Omkar-Brahma assumes physical, corporal and other forms. Gradually he will realise that *Omkar-Naad* alone is playing, assuming all these forms. With the dawning of this knowledge, the disease of seeing many is cured. Then he meditates on the thought 'I pervade everything' and loses all perception of the existence of a second. The *sadhaka*, thereafter, crosses easily the *samsara* with its dangers of life and death.

364. The three *mantras* (component parts) of *Omkara* (A, U, Ma), if contemplated independently of one another and without the knowledge of the Person (*brahman*), are mortal and the effects produced is destructible. Worshippers of *Omkara* contemplated in this way, cannot conquer death. But if a man

combines (harmonises) these three *mantras* properly as a whole (*Omkara*) and connects them with the different phases of the Person (*Brahman*) who presides over the three states (wakefulness, dream and deep dreamless sleep), and meditates on these phases as systematically related to one another, he is to be regarded as a worshipper who has true insight into the nature of *Omkara* and he is not agitated by the thought of death.

7

NAAM

365. People love Baba (Sitaramdas Omkarnath) in the same proportion as they sing *Naam*; your Baba loves *Naam* dearly. Forever and ever sing *Naam*[1] to Him.

366. To chant *Naam* is to do great service to Sitaram. Consider your self to be akin to a blade of grass. As you sing *Naam*, earn the virtue of tolerance shown by a blade of grass.

367. Chant *Naam*, you will have peace; you will become immortal. Chant *Naam*, you will be free from the cycle of birth and death. Chant *Naam*, because I tell you to do it, chant *Naam* knowing that I am listening.

368. 'I' am no different from *Naam*; sustain the *Naam* on the tongue, in your breath, in the mind, in the heart, uphold *Naam* everywhere, drown yourself in *Naam*,

---

1 *Tarak Brahma Naam* viz. *Hare Krishna Hare Krishna Krishna Krishna Hare Hare, Hare Ram Hare Ram Ram Ram Hare Hare*

only then will you be able to live in my heart and all the burning pain will cool down.

Naam, the Kali Yuga Remedy

369. In this *yuga*, there is no other way than taking refuge in Him and chanting *Naam*. 'I take refuge in you', 'I am at your mercy, protect me!' – reciting this *mahamantra* and chanting *Naam* while sitting and standing, eating and lying down – this alone is the supreme remedy.

370. In *Kali Yuga* one of the most accessible, simple, easy, joyous and incomparable means of welfare of the world is to steadfastly take refuge in *Naam-Sundara*[2]. Name (of God) and God are one and the same.

371. The means to attain *bhakti* (devotion) is *Naam*; it helps grant salvation to individuals in *Kali Yuga;* that is why the virtuous, as well as those adept at perceiving the essence, highly revere *Kali Yuga*. Beings of other *yugas* desire to be born in *Kali Yuga*.

872. *Naamkirtan* alone is the way in *Kali Yuga*. The specially qualified one gets more from writing *Naam* than from *kirtan;* he is freed from incurable maladies.

373. To know that there is *Brahma* is *paroksha jnana* but the knowledge that 'I am *Brahma*, is *aparoksha* or direct knowledge. In order to acquire this *jnana*

---

2 Beautiful name (of God)

(knowledge), one has to have faith in the words of the *Sat-Guru* and the *Shastras*. A *Sat-Guru* is difficult to get and in this difficult age, how many persons are fortunate enough to read the *Vedas* and the Scriptures? It is doubtful if even one amongst a thousand have this facility. A *bhakta*, whose desire is to gain *paramananda* (eternal bliss), can attain it easily by singing *Hari-Naam*.

Tarak Brahma Naam

374. *Hare Krishna Mantra* has its foundation in the *Vedas*, *Tantras* and *Puranas*. Sri Mahaprabhu preached this *Naam*. This is the *Naam*-deliverer of *Kali Yuga*.

375. The path of *Naam samkirtana* is simple, straight and easily reached. The splendour of My Name transcends even that of the *Vedas* and *Vedanta*. Those who forever sing the Name of God are equally worshipped in all three worlds. Their blessing delivers the sinful and afflicted.

376. There's as much bliss as you sing *Naam*!
There's as much bliss as you sing Naam!
There's as much bliss as you sing *Naam*!
Hare Krishna Hare Krishna Krishna Krishna Hare Hare
Hare Ram Hare Ram Ram Ram Hare Hare

377. If you sing a great deal of *Naam*, great deal of bliss will come to your lot. There's as much bliss to be enjoyed as you chant *Naam*.

378. To seek authentic welfare of every devotee, and to bless them, preach the adoption of *Tarak Brahma Naam: Hare Krishna Hare Krishna Krishna Krishna Hare Hare, Hare Ram Hare Ram Ram Ram Hare Hare,* may it be sung to the accompaniment of *khol* and *kartaal*[3] and with dance. That is enough. This alone will manifest the *Anahat Naad*[4].

Singing *Naam* Aloud

379. By singing *Naam* loudly the birds and the beasts, plants and trees, are all sanctified (by listening to *Naam*), the *naamkari*[5] is also sanctified. There's one more thing: normally only those who are in close vicinity hear *Naam*, but by singing it loudly *Naam* mixes with the air and reaches those who are even five hundred feet afar. It sanctifies the atmosphere, the distant ones are blessed, and breathing in this charged air, their hearts are purified.

Naam is Easy ~ it's for Everyone

380. People talk of *vairagya, vairagya, vairagya*[6]. There is no necessity of *vairagya*. You stay as you are and only try to sing the *Naam*. *Naam* is God. If once you can hold on to Him, then no anxiety should come to your mind. The man, who stays with the King,

---

3 The wooden or metallic clapper used in Indian devotional music
4 Unstruck Sound – the sound of the cosmos, which exists by itself without friction
5 Chanter of *Naam*
6 Detachment from the pleasures of this world and of heaven

does not ask for favors from the doorkeepers. The man, whose tongue does not relish *Ram Naam*, let him think of *vairagya*.

381. *Naam* is definitely a great spiritual practice, but it is not difficult at all. It is something which children, old men, young boys and girls, everyone can do. By adopting *Naam*, one can be rid of sorrow, disease, distress and suffering. This is a practice that embodies the essence of various *sadhanas* (spiritual practices).

382. First of all, crave for *satsang*, the company of holy men – that will help you develop interest in *Naam*. Thereafter, strive to chant *Naam* all the time. In the beginning you may not be able to do it, even if you do slip, never mind. Seek the company of holy men and once again give yourself to *Naam samkirtan* and *japa* enthusiastically. Chanting 'Durga, Durga, Durga', your mind will be purified. And you will be able to chant *Naam* regularly.

Ram *Naam*

383. There is no one who is free from physical or mental disorders. Nor is there anyone who is free from all wants. That is why it is necessary for everyone to repeat 'Ram, Ram'. Ram *Naam* means Name of God. Whichever Name (of the deity) has been given by one's Guru, by repeating that very Name, man succeeds in reaching the destination.

384. Self-restraint and sacred texts establish a man in supreme bliss. He, who is good for nothing and cannot undertake to purify food habits, cannot seek association of holy men, nor do any worship, the way for such a person is Ram *Naam*.

385. There is no reason for you to be anxious. It is true that Ratnakar had *vairagya*, but he could not utter Ram *Naam*; so he did *japa* of Mara *Naam*. You have not got *vairagya*; you have lust, anger and attachment; but your asset is that you can utter Ram *Naam*; then why will you not attain *param gati*? Have you committed any sin of abortion, robbery and sexual intercourse with some other's wife? If not, why are you anxious? You are not a murderer of *Brahmins*, you are not a robber, you do not go after others' wives, and you can chant Ram *Naam*. Only thing you don't have is *vairagya*. Do not bother about *vairagya*; practice chanting *Naam*.

386. By chanting 'Ram Ram', all the time, you will get whatever you desire. Wealth, prosperity, fame etc. will roll at your feet even if you don't desire them. Just make the attempt to chant 'Ram Ram' always.

387. Ram *Naam* is the supreme doctrine and knowledge, the supreme absorption among meditations, and supreme *yoga* system.

388. *Japa* of 'Ram' can be undertaken by Shaivites, Vaishnavas, *shaktas*...everyone. This is the *mantra* which Uma Maheshwara[7] constantly chants; it is *mantra* that fortifies religious sentiments of every order of devotees.

389. It is possible to win His grace by chanting 'Ram, Ram' while sitting and standing, eating and lying down. There is no doubt about this. Those desirous of God's grace can test this out on their own.

390. If one keeps uttering 'Ram Ram', one will be saved the trouble of practicing *dhyana*. To attain *dhyana* one will not have to take recourse to imagery. *Naam* itself will cross the uttered and silent states of meditation and start playing in the mind.

391. Mental *japa* is itself *dhyana*; for this, one does not require any imagery or blind faith. If one keeps repeating Ram *Naam* constantly, the *Naam* gets inextricably mixed into his bones and marrow, his blood and flesh. The current of *Naam* passes through every vein and artery in his body. *Naam* starts playing in his seven hundred and seventy-two million odd veins. Five hundred and forty million odd hairs on his body start dancing. Then God appears before him in person and blesses him.

---

7 Lord Shiva

Shabda Brahma

392. This world is created from *shabda* (sound); whatever
is visible outside is the manifestation of compact mass
of *Shabda*. Inside, the same *shabda* or *naad* sports, in
the form of *para* in the anal region, *pashyanti* in the
navel, *madhyama* in the heart and *vaikhari* in the
tongue. This *shabda* is indeed God.

Nature of Naam

393. It is true that by partaking of the nectar of immortality
which rose from the churning of the ocean, the gods
attained immortality. Their sorrows, anguish and
troubles, however, did not cease. But those who
partake of the nectar of God's Name, superior by far,
are rid of all the worries pertaining to this world and
the next. They are forever drowned in the ocean of
bliss. They experience the bliss instinct with total
divine consciousness, and though living in the world,
they are not tainted by worldliness. For them, the
entire world is God manifest; they cannot perceive
anything except God.

394. In the same way as the Lord incarnated as *matsya*
(fish) and rescued the sages and holy men and
destroyed evil-doers, *Naam* too is a singular
incarnation of the Lord. He is incarnated as the *vastra*
(garment) in the court of the Kauravas to defend
the modesty of Draupadi; He incarnated in Gokul
in the form of *vatsa* and *gopa* (cowherd) to rid

Brahma of his infatuation; He descended in the form of *kurma* (tortoise) to support the Mandara mountain at the churning of the ocean; in the same way He assumed *Naam avatara* to deliver mankind (from the ocean of *samsara*).

395. Goswami Tulasidas has said, *Naam* is greater than both *saguna* and *nirguna* Brahma. *Naam*, with its power, has brought both types of Brahma under its subjection.

396. Everything in this world is *asat* (unreal), only *Naam* is *sat* (real).

397. There is but one single entity – it is seen as a form with the eyes, ears hear it, skin touches it, and the tongue tastes it. The entity is but one. It can be experienced with the help of *Naam*.

398. Recite *Naam*, my mind! without a break
And thou wilt find peace and conquer death.
From the name has this universe arise,
In the Name all objects find their support.
The Name objectifies itself into the world,
The Name becomes all forms of life and moves.

399. As man, woman, bird, beast, worm and insect.
The Name in myriad forms enjoys its sport
Manifesting itself as day, as night,

As half month and month and the six seasons
The Name is all: it is the sun, the moon,
The planets; the Name is light and darkness.
The basis off all things is the Name,
It is river, hill and sea, tree and creeper.
Remember Rama, sing Rama, Rama,
And thou wilt attain bliss, O Sitaram!

400. The *Shastras* have proclaimed it loudly – other than the inferior pleasure of the senses, there is a great joy on earth which is sublime and supreme. This very body can experience it; it can be obtained in this *yuga* only through chanting of *Naam*.

Shravan & Kirtan

401. In *shravana* (listening to *Naam*) only *shravana* is achieved, but in *kirtan* (singing) you have the benefit of both *shravana* and *kirtana*, therefore *kirtana* is considered superior.

402. The root lies in *shravana* (listening to *Naam*). The tongue of the sinner is incapable of singing *Naam*. After having recourse with *shravana* (listening to *Naam*) repeatedly, when the sins deplete, then the tongue gains the power to sing *Naam*.

403. Extremely sinful ones do not even have the fortune of *shravana* (listening to *Naam*). These people stay far away from any contact with God. If somehow

Naam manages to reach their ears, it attracts them by dint of its own force.

404. You are listening to God's lore; if you will remember God while listening to His divine sports, you will gain more joy. To forget Him and to recite things inanely gives no joy.

Sufficiency of *Naam*

405. Do not be disheartened with apprehension that impure thoughts will lead to an offence in your *Naam* (*sadhana*). *Naam* itself will confer upon you the strength to chant *Naam*; it will destroy all your sins and give you a new lease of life.

406. Let obstructions come, like the Vindya Hills[8], obstructing the path to the south, let difficulties obstruct your way of *bhajan*, but undaunted you carry on your *Naam-kirtan* and do not abandon it. Like dry leaves before a storm, these mountains of difficulties will also be blown away, for ever. *Naam* is not a simple thing. In *Naam* lies hidden an enormous strength.

407. People who are capable of chanting *Naam* continuously need to undertake no other spiritual practice. But how many can be so fortunate? That is the reason *Gayatri japa*, at the three prescribed

---

8 The Vindhya range comprises old, rounded mountains and hills in the west-central Indian sub-continent

hours, *japa* of the *Ishta mantra* and reading of the sacred texts extolling the divine sport, need to be undertaken daily.

408. Those who take refuge with *Naam* and try to conduct themselves righteously according to their ability, they entertain merely the desire: 'I will forever adhere to Naam'; they don't have to worry about doing anything else. These are the people I hold close to my heart.

409. Listen. My Name is your support in the journey of life. Sing *Naam*. Today you are alive, but you will not be alive forever. A day will come when your senses will cease to function and life will leave the corporal frame, and the mortal remains will be either devoured by jackals or burnt to ashes. If you do not obtain the means of support for the journey, then you are doomed. From this moment – sing *Naam*; let your whole system utter the words 'Rama Rama' and 'Hari Hari'. This is the best means of leading you to the right path in life. Your wealth, your wife and children will not go with you. While there is still time, sing *Naam* and obtain what is most worth your while in life. Don't follow too many paths to the higher life, better stick to one – the singing of *Naam* – this will be the best of your attainments. You need not be proficient in all the scriptures.

Power of *Naam*

410. Even today a man can attain God by chanting *Naam*.
I don't say it just once; I avow it a hundred times,
thousand times, a million or zillion times that even
now men can see God.

411. Keep chanting *Naam* always and blow away the
frenzied tensions of the mind, and difficulties (which
the scriptures report), on the path of spirituality, with
the help of the *Naam*-cannon.

412. With the cannon of *Naam*, blow away all your
deficiencies, disturbances, grief, unhappiness, disease,
and distress; carry on unpurturbed. Sitting or
standing, eating or sleeping, sing *Naam*. Victory to
Naam! Victory to *Naam*! *Charaiva iti charaiva iti* –
march on; keep moving ahead! Jai Sitaram!

413. Sing *Naam*. *Naam* alone is the great net to catch the
prana. By singing *Naam* a devotee can succeed in
taking *prana* to *prananath* (lord of the breath) and
make even God his eternal companion.

414. Once you take refuge with *Naam*, there is nothing
to worry about. The waves of the ocean of *samsara*
will recede now.

Naam Satisfies Desire

415. *Naam* is the wish-yielding tree. Whatever you desire of it, you will get it. You will surely get it. If anyone sings *Naam* with one wish in mind, a hundred are fulfilled.

416. Are you crying due to the grief due to lack of food, clothes and money? Sing *Naam*, sing *Naam*! Whether you desire it or not, food will be heaped at your doors, you will be able to feed thousands of people. Without seeking it, lots of money will fall at your feet. You will not have to worry about clothes; in fact, you will be able to distribute clothes to other people. Even if you want to renounce it, the objects and wealth you are indifferent to, will follow you. I am in no way exaggerating. Should you require proof, come to me I can give you a testimony of this.

417. *Hare Krishna Hare Krishna Krishna Krishna Hare Hare, Hare Ram Hare Ram Ram Ram Hare Hare*: keep chanting this *mahamantra* continuously. You will not have to worry about anything; God will take care of your entire burden. He will look after your needs; you will be free of all tensions. Just keep chanting *Naam*. Don't let a single breath be wasted.

Naam is too Powerful for Worldly Good, Sins...

418. Repentance, austerities, reading holy texts and giving charity during times beset with difficulties, even these can exhaust one's sins. Therefore, it is inappropriate

to take refuge with *Naam* for the purpose of destroying one's sins. Sins are destroyed automatically in the process of *Naam* chanting. 'God, be thou pleased with me!' this is the sentiment a devotee must harbour in mind while adopting *Naam*. One doesn't need to summon an elephant in rut to kill a mosquito!

419. It is possible for a supplicant to get the desired object through *Naam*. But those who sit beneath the wish-yielding tree of *Naam* and seek worldly pleasures; they are deprived of the ultimate good. *Naam* satisfies their desires; it does not reveal its supremely blissful nature of truth to them.

420. He who enthrones *Naam* on the *asana* (seat) once, he doesn't have to think of anything; the second seat is naturally taken by God. Wealth rolls at the feet of he who sings *Naam*.

How Fast Does *Naam* Work?

421. Do you know how *Naam* works? If you set a pile of wood on fire just once, the fire turns it into ashes. There is no need to set it on fire again and again. In the same way, if anyone utters my Name once, his tongue becomes *vaishnavi*. Thereafter it cannot rest for a moment without chanting *Naam*; this indeed is the secret of *Naam*.

422. If a single matchstick can burn hundreds of haystacks, if it can burn hundreds of kilos of cottonwool; if a small little matchstick can turn the darkness of a terrible mountain cave into light, in a trice, why can't a human being attain salvation by chanting the *Chidatmak Naam*[9]? *Naam* itself is God.

423. He, who is a grave sinner, if he sings *Naam*, his sins burn away slowly like the haystack. He who is a common sinner, his sins burn away rapidly, like the heap of cottonwool. As for the virtuous man, if he chants *Naam*, the dark cave of the heart is instantly filled with brightness. It is *Naam* alone that works in mild, medium, and intense variation, depending upon the differences in individuals.

424. One utterance of *Naam* is enough to set on fire the heap of sins of a grave sinner. It keeps burning. More chanting of the *Naam* acts like like a breeze that fans the fire. The sins are burnt away rapidly. Futile talk other than *Naam* interrupts the salutable process, it is like showers obstructing fire, then it takes a while longer burn – but there is no power in the world which can put out the conflagration of *Naam* once ignited.

425. If the chanter of *Naam* is a great sinner, in evil company, indiscriminate in his dietary habits, given

---

9 Name in the form of Soul and of the nature of wisdom.

to womanising and of easy virtue, it takes a long time for him to obtain the effect of *Naam*.

426. Conversely, if the chanter of *Naam* is of virtuous company, fond of *sattvik* food, a follower of the path outlined by the *Shastras* (scriptures) and eschews of female company, he gains the experiences quickly.

Operation of *Naam*

427. Every single letter of *Naam* is *jyotirmaya*[10] and *jyotirbindu*[11]. *Naam* penetrates into us through our eyes, ears, nose, and from every pore of one's body. It's like an injection; *Naam* helps pay off the debt owed to the *rishis*.

428. As you say *Ra* the mouth opens and sin goes out: as you say *M*, the mouth closes and sin can't enter again. Then dive right into *madhyama*; dive again and you reach *pahsyanti*; dive yet again and you come straight to *para*.

429. The singer of *Naam* sacrifices both sin and merit. By hearing *Naam* constantly, the Mother [*kundalini*] is awakened. Then she starts singing and dancing, emanating light both inside and outside the singer [She comes in the form of *Nada*]. The singer of *Naam* then keeps hearing this spontaneous singing by the Mother. In the brilliant light of the Mother's body,

---

10 Divinely effulgent
11 Locus of supraconscious awareness in the form of effulgence

the singer sees the *devayana* – the road to *vaikuntha*. At the time of departing from this life, he discards his outer frame and goes out by the Brahma-*randhara* and this liberated soul goes along the *devayana*, where he is worshipped by the gods and finally arrives at *vaikuntha*, at the feet of *Sri Bhagawan*, who lifts him up and endears him.

430. For whatever duration of time you keep the 'iron' of your mind in the 'fire' of My Name, it (your mind) will remain as hot as fire itself and have the power of destroying all the sins of the world. Afterwards, when you withdraw from *Naam* and squat lazily, the breeze of enjoyment, of pleasure, will blow over your mind and turn it cold – the 'iron' will once again become cold as before.

431. Is it possible to gain freedom by chanting Hari *Naam* just once? No matter how, but once you sing Hari *Naam*, then *Naam* itself doesn't leave you. Thereafter, *Naam* never leaves you and willy-nilly, you are made to continue chanting as if by hypnosis. Even if you say, 'I will give up *Naam*', even then *Naam* doesn't leave you.

432. If a person were to merely continue to sing *Naam* orally, *Naam* has such power as would give him the strength to recite *Naam* with the body, mind and speech within a short period of time.

433. There is no doubt, whoever sings *Naam* or performs *Naam-japa*, he will attain the blessed state; continuing to chant *Naam*, when the body, mind and the *prana* become one with *Naam*, it is possible for a *naami* (chanter of *Naam*) to attain God or the *Omkar Shabda Brahma*[12].

434. The principal actor and director of the drama of this world is God, He alone is enacting the whole drama with His Inseparable-Consort; there is nothing else in the world. A devotee can fully realize this truth while chanting *Naam*.

435. One must sing *Naam* and conquer *prana*; *jiva-bhava* (sense of individuality) is nothing but the restlessness of *prana*. Gradually, as the *prana* becomes still, man attains divine objects beyond this world, when the *prana* begins to dwell within the nose and is internalized, liberation is attained.

436. Whether *Naam* is sung loudly or in low tones, Sitaram purifies the chanter by attracting his *paramanus*[13]. His body becomes pure.

437. When you chant *Naam*, as you stand or sit, eat or go to bed, you will realize everyone is sunk in God in the same way as the fish resides in water. *Naam! Naam! Naam!*

---

12 Word-God; *Brahman* in the form of sound; *Omkara* or the *Veda*
13 Particles or vibrations

438. All bodily sins are destroyed by dancing to the accompaniment of *kirtan*[14] instantly; the spring of *sattva* courses through the body and mind.

Call Out

439. Standing and sitting, eating or lying down, always repeat, 'Ram', Ram' or the Name of your chosen deity. As long as you feel God is away, call Him loudly. When you feel He is close by, call him softly and gently.

440. After a while calling out will stop on its own. He (God) will call you. When that happens, throw the honour and prestige of your family to the winds, and jump into the universal ocean with inevitable urge. Aha! What a great flood of bliss!

441. One calls out loudly for someone who is far; as for someone who is near, there's no need to shout – this is a precept straight from the saint's tongue. Now, call out internally, within your mind.

The Inevitable Effect of *Naam*

442. If you chant *Naam*, you do not have to desire for *mukti*, it comes as a maid to serve you.

443. Chant *Naam*, just keep singing and chanting *Naam*. Before you realize it, you will attain oneness with Me, all your quest will end.

---

14 Singing, chanting the Name of God, His praise or *Mahamantra*

444. The physical powers do not depend on faith or lack of faith for their operation – the body burns even if you pour nitric acid on it without faith; if you put your hand in fire with disdain, it is nevertheless burnt. Even as death is inevitable though the poison is consumed without faith, *Naam* accomplishes the salvation of every man irrespective of the nature of its adoption.

445. *Naam* is like burning mustard seeds, the way mustard seeds pull out the snake no matter where it is; *Naam* draws back the mind from wherever it may be.

446. Those who take recourse to *Naam* do not eat anything except the remains of offerings made to God, which is why their diet automatically becomes *sattvik* (pure). As they continue to sing *Naam* all the time, *Naam* dispels carnal desires, thus both *sattvik* diet and *brahmacharya* are automatically achieved.

447. One takes refuge with *Naam* in order to cultivate *prema* (love). Just as it is unnecessary to tell the sun: 'Sir, please dispel darkness,' for as soon as the sun rises the darkness is naturally dispelled, similarly, as soon as the desire, 'I will take refuge with *Naam*,' arises in the heart, the sins automatically depart. Thus it is not necessary to resolve on depleting one's sins by adopting *Naam*. (It follows naturally!)

448. All right! I won't ask you to believe blindly – undertake to *sing Naam* seriously for an hour in the morning and an hour at night for one month – you will yourself realize the greatness of *Naam*.

449. If a wicked person sings *Naam* in order to earn fame among people, *Naam* grants him fame all right, but because of his excessive wickedness, he has to undergo penalty as well.

450. When you dance while singing *Hari Naam*, the bodily sins are destroyed. As soon as the sins are destroyed, *Naad*[15] and *Jyoti*[16] manifest. Several people have experienced *Naad* and *Jyoti* while singing *Naam*; they didn't have to take recourse to dense forests or mountain caves.

451. Chant *Naam Samkirtana* while dancing. This will destroy the sins accumulated over many lives. Dancing with *Naam* quickly purges sins incurred with the body.

452. Sitaram is not tempting you. If you wish to have proof, Sitaram will give you sure evidence that by chanting 'Ram Ram', a human being can be revered among people.

453. Is it possible to abandon such a big world and surge and drown in the mighty ocean of bliss, measureless

---

15 Divine Sound
16 Divine light, effulgence

in every direction, just with a single sermon? Hard as it may seem, have recourse to chanting 'Ram Ram'. God will conduct you (to bliss). If it were possible to gain God-realization with a single sermon, there would be *brahmajnani* in every home. One has to put in hard work – try with all one's might.

Naam & Ashraddha

454. There is no rule or command saying you must adopt chanting of *Naam* only after you have become truthful and your mind is purified; even the rank criminals can purify their mind by chanting *Naam* and become truthful. In this awful and terrible *Kali Yuga* who but *Naam* can purify the mind? Chant *Naam* with or without faith – you are bound to gain God's grace.

455. You do not have to wait to develop the taste. Whether you have the taste or not, whether you like it or not, do not look back or sideways, but go on singing *Naam*.

456. My name is Govinda, you are calling out 'Govinda, Govinda,' absent-mindedly; do you think I won't answer your call? Do you think I won't come to you? Even if I come close to you and discover that you are calling me absent-mindedly – even then I will say, 'O brother! I have come!' Even if you call Him absent-mindedly, He still comes to you laughing and says, 'O brother! See, I have come!'

457. With emotion or without emotion, with faith or without faith, or even to gain fame as a holy man, whichever way *Naam* is chanted, *Naam* helps the chanter to cross the ocean of worldly existence.

458. Whether with belief or disbelief, or even if one sings My *Naam* with disdain, My *Naam Omkar* is ever ingrained in his heart. *Naam* grants its grace upon everyone irrespective of belief; man is blessed whichever way *Naam* is heard or uttered by him.

459. As long as there is no spiritual experience, the devotion may not be complete. But even if devoid of belief, trusting in Guru's words, one must pursue *Naam*; it is *Naam* that bestows experience eventually.

460. There is no harm in singing *Naam kirtan* aloud. In fact, it achieves great welfare. But if someone preaches *Naam* to a disbeliever, he is not only likely to ignore it, but also blaspheme *Naam*, defile his tongue and get the preacher of *Naam* as well to partake of the sin by getting him to listen to the defamation of *Naam*. It is for this reason, he who preaches to a disbeliever is considered guilty.

461. Brother! Ratnakara repeated 'Mara, Mara' in *japa* and attained; Ajamil called out to his son Narayana and attained Narayana Himself. If that is the case, why won't you get the fruit of calling Him absent-mindedly?

No *Naam* is Lost

462. Well, what happens to those who sing a lot of *Naam* for few days and then give it up? Does the sum of all the *Naam* they have sung earlier come to nothing? No... No! Not a single *Naam* is lost. Every *Naam* that a man listens to or utters, is mixed with his flesh, blood, bones and nerves, it fuses with atoms and molecules of the body and is stored; when the *punya karmas*[17] rise, the fresh *Naam* that's sung adds up to the accumulated stock and enhances his *Naam* credit balance.

Experiences of *Naam*

463. With the help of *Naam kirtan* it is possible to obtain *Bindu* and *Naad* (*anaahatadhwanih aatmanirghoshah*[18]) easily. The devotee, having lost himself in singing *Naam Samkirtan*, takes refuge in God and completely surrendering his body, mind and all, lives in this world while being His. He doesn't have to worry about anything thereafter.

464. The day you feel that the photograph of Guruji is Guruji Himself, that day the photo will speak with you. As long as you think it's just a photograph, there will be no experience.

---

17 Meritorious and virtuous deeds
18 The self- initiated (unstruck) sound is the sound of the soul (*Atman*)

465. When you notice that people are involuntarily being attracted to a holy man, you must understand that this holy man has attained *Jyoti*[19], *Naad*. It is certain he is exclusively devoted to God.

Unbroken Remembrance of *Naam*

466. Don't give up chanting of *Naam*. Don't give your tongue even a minute of rest from chanting *Naam*. Just as there are flood and ebb tides in Ganga, there are floods and ebbs in the world of spiritual practice too. But there is nothing to worry. *Ma Bhaih*! Fear not! Since you have sought refuge with Sitaram, if Sitaram is to attain to final happiness, you too would make it to the same goal.

467. Keep repeating 'Ram, Ram'; you are bound to find peace. Just as it is certain that the night follows day and life is followed by death, in the same manner, it's true that *naamkaris* (chanters of *Naam*) obtain peace. This is a truth, perfect truth, and a truth evermore! Jai Sitaram!

468. Repeat 'Durga, Durga', forever and ever. That will take care of all your *sadhana*. Nothing is gained by trying to jump to greatness. How can mere parroting of big words from the scriptures alleviate suffering?

---

19 Divine light, effulgence

469. Those who are capable of chanting *Naam* ceaselessly, are automatically and lovingly ferried across to His abode by *Naam* itself. *Naam Samkirtan* purifies the moveable and immoveable world. It gives a new lease of energy.

Naam Upakaar ~ Benevolence of *Naam*

470. Those who are attempting to do welfare to the world should do at least three hours of *Naam Samkirtan* every day. The Human being does not come into the world for himself. He is born for the welfare of others.

471. Whether solicited or not, do ultimate good unto people and oneself by calling out people and imploring them to chant *Naam*. May the atmosphere everywhere be sanctified with *Naam*!

472. How will you become a devotee? Standing and sitting, eating or lying down, always repeat 'Durga, Durga' or 'Sitaram, Sitaram' …do it, you will surely become a devotee.

Naam Ananda ~ Bliss

473. When the *sattvik bhava* is crystallized, *prema* (love) is developed. When *prema* arises, the world appears imbued with God.

474. Every devotee will receive, as much bliss as he progresses on the path – there can be no doubt in this regard! If you want bliss, progress more and more in chanting *Naam*.

475. *Ananda* (bliss) is in one's own fist. The name of God is nothing but a bundled mass of *ananda*; there's as much bliss in store for the *naami* (chanter) as he chants it.

476. Devotion and love of chanting *Naam* is not an ordinary thing; unless a man has a store of virtue accumulated over many lives, desire to sing *Naam* does not arise.

477. Those who can always chant the *Naam*, standing or sitting, eating or resting, in pure or impure condition, are the only ones who will get the nectar of contentment and be blessed.

478. Practice unbroken *Naam japa*; that will give you supreme bliss.

Naam versus Naami ~ Name & the Named

479. For how long does a singer of *Naam* get the vision of *the naami* (God)? He gets a vision for a split second and then God disappears. But *Naam* is not like that, it lays hold of you eternally, it does not wax or wane. *Naam* is an eternal companion – a companion of the heart! That's the reason *Naam* is greater than *the Naami*.

480. Thakur's *Naam* is greater than Thakur. You will gain Him in whichever form you desire – *saguna* or *nirguna* (with or without name, form and attributes)

481. *Naam* and *Naami* are not different[20]. To keep chanting 'Krishna, Krishna', and to live with Krishna is quite the same thing. Just keep calling him while standing or sitting, eating or lying down, with or without discipline, with faith or with disdain – just call Him!

Naam as medium for *Sadhana* ~ Spiritual Practice

482. *Naam* is the life of all *karmas*. It is meaningless to undertake charity and other *vratas*[21] without chanting *Naam*. Charity, observances, austerities, sacrifices and offerings to the *pitris*[22] etc. are all fruitless without *Naam*. People, who perform virtuous deeds, gain infinite fruit from them when they are performed along with *Naam Sankirtan*; with *Naam* they reach their goal speedily.

483. Chanting *Naam* is nothing but the preliminary stage of *dhyana* or meditation. One can gain the fruit of *dhyana* through chanting *Naam*. When *the Naam* trickles down from *vaikhari* (audible sound rooted in the tongue) to *madhyama* (sound akin to whispering in the heart region), one reaches the state of meditation automatically.

---

20 In *Naam* resides the *Naami* or the being. Within the *mantra* lives the *chaitanya* or consciousness; both are identical.
21 *Vrata* denotes 'religious vow'. It involves performance of any ritual voluntarily over a particular period of time
22 The fathers, ancestors, the spirits of the departed

Mauna, Control of Speech & Naam

484. *Shabda Brahman, Omkar,* holds the body up as *para, pashyanti, madhyama* and *vaikhari*[23]. *Para* is at the anal region, *pashyanti* at the navel, *madhyama* at the heart and *vaikhari* at the tongue. The universe is *shabda* or *vaani* all over. That indeed is God. To restrain *vaani* is to get to the centre of being all too easily. Its normal course (*anuolm gati*) is *para, pashyanti, madhyama, vaikhari,* while its inverted order (*vilom gati*) is *vaikhari, madhyama, pashyanti, para. Para* is the Supreme who is existence, consciousness and bliss together (*satchitananda ghana*).

485. Until you are not free from worldly bondage, it is good to observe *mauna*[24] for two to five hours every day. Gradually, one must extend this from five to seven days at a stretch and practice *nadanusandhan*[25]. It is possible to gain peace like this. Thereafter, observing *mauna* for indefinite period of time, one can attain the blessed goal.

23 The four kinds of *vaak* or speech; sprouting in para, *vaak* (power of speech) gives forth two leaves in *pashyanti*, buds forth in *madhyama* and blossoms in *vaikhari*, that *vaak* reaches the stage of the absorption of sound. *Vaikhari* is the gross quality of the vocal organs, *madhyama* is the subtler quality of the same physical organs, *pashyanti* is the quality of the subconscious or unconscious, and *para* is the quality of the soul. *Para* is transcendental sound, still and infinite of the nature of *jyoti* (light); *pashyanti* is mental sound, subconscious; *madhyama* is middle sound, a sound produced in whispering; *vaikahri* is audible, producible and spoken sound. To sum up, *vaikhari* is the gross quality of the vocal organs, *madhyama* is the subtler quality of the same physical organs, *pashyanti* is the quality of the subconscious or unconscious, and *para* is the quality of the soul.
24 Vow of silence
25 Practice of fixing one's attention upon the inner sound in order to bring about the dissolution of mental modifications (*chitta vrittis*), this, as sage Patanjali describes, leads to *laya* (absorption)

486. It is God who sports in the form of *vaak* (speech). The more a man speaks, the farther he goes from God.

487. Repeating 'Ram, Ram', if it is possible to enter within, while observing *mauna* (silence), one can even reach God. *Mauna* is a great spiritual instrument.

488. Through the practice of *mauna*, the mind is directed inwards. It is not possible to keep pace with the outside world (and enter within).

489. Without control of speech, nothing is possible. The mind cannot be directed inwards without this.

Naam & Drashta Bhava ~ Witness Attitude

490. Even if you don't derive pleasure, you can still live with *drashta bhava* (witness attitude) repeating 'Ram! Ram! Ram!' Do you know how? Supposing you are saying 'Ram! Ram! Ram!' and suddenly a thought crops up in your mind: 'I can't get up in the mornings. Ram! Ram! Ram!' 'When I don't get up early in the morning, my day's work is spoiled. Ram! Ram! Ram!' 'But I must find a way to get up early in the morning. Ram! Ram! Ram!' In this way, all the resolves and uncertainties envisaged by the mind roll in, and disappear like pictures in a cinema, and the trick of the mind is caught. It becomes clear that 'I' am different from the mind. But in a state bereft of *Naam*, the mind has the capacity to tranquilize you with its resolves and misgivings.

491. Ratnakar could not even pronounce Ram *Naam*; he achieved his end by chanting 'Mara, Mara.' Ajamila, at the time of his death, saw the messengers of Yama and desperately called out for his son Narayana and was liberated by this *Naam-abhaas*[26].

Naam & Patan Fall

492. Why is it that people fall even after taking refuge with *Naam*? The principal reason for fall is bad *prarabddha*[27]. Despite the fact *prarabddha* makes the person fall, *Naam* lifts him up afresh.

Pranaam ~ Salutation or Obeisance

493. Your mind must not be attached to any object of this world. It must be fixed on the Lotus Feet of that One Supreme Being. As long as you think in terms of 'my' and 'mine', you will have to undergo the endless cycle of births and deaths; you will have to endure happiness and misery, since till then the *samsara* remains. Once you do away with your desires and cravings – you will be free and you will attain an emancipated life.

494. Practice obeisance, the greatest prayer and worship (*sadhdana*), is to prostrate yourself before everybody and all objects, assuming them to be the Guru – be it good or bad, virtuous or wicked, auspicious or inauspicious, beautiful or ugly, pleasant or unpleasant.

---

26 A semblance of *Naam*, just a reflection of consciousness as against *Shuddha* or real *Naam*

27 Portion of past *karma* which is responsible for the present body, karma that has matured or neared fruition

495. *Maam Namaskuru* – pay obeisance unto Me – is the greatest maxim of *Sri Gita*. There is no better *sadhana* than this.

496. Always offer *pranaam* – this way, no matter who you are, and how much impurity there is in you, you will still attain to Me. You will surely reach Me; that's certain! I give my unfailing assurance that I will appear in your vision, I will surely reveal Myself to you.

497. *Pranaam* means *Na Mam*('not mine' or 'this body is not mine'). Lord! This is your body. Sacrificing oneself thus, the sins are destroyed; God's compassion rains down … Ram! Ram! Sitaram!

498. It is our duty to offer *pranaam*. In the case of those who will not let you touch their feet, bow before them from a distance. (That is why they say it is always good to offer *pranaam* to everyone from a little distance). It is our duty to offer *pranaam*, and we must always do it.

499. 'Everyone is a part of the vast body of God', mentally contemplating thus, practice offering *pranaam* to all. He alone is disguised in everything. Human beings see friend and enemy, good and evil, due to the vision marred by one's sins.

500. If possible, bow down in obeisance to the elders three times daily. 'Everything is a part of God's body'– thinking thus, one must make it a practice to offer *pranaam* to all objects.

501. When people look at a holy man and offer *pranaam* to him, if the holy man returns a glance, the *sattvik*[28] current in his body purifies the one who offers a *pranaam*, with a mere glance.

502. He who obtains a sight of anything holy has his sins destroyed; that is the reason *pranaam* is made. The *sattvik* currents pass into him in proportion to the deference he shows (to the holy entity).

503. A *pranaam* that involves full prostration helps a holy man see and bless the entire body. His sight purifies the entire body of the supplicant. The merit and purification is reduced, to the extent body is revealed when bent on knees, and further reduced, when one joins palms to offer *pranaam*.

504. God can be realized easily. *Pranaam*! *Pranaam*! If you can offer just *pranaam*, you need to do nothing more. God declares in the *Gita* – '*maam namaskuru* (offer obeisance unto me)'.

---

28 Vibrations of purity and goodness

505. To worship and realize God with mere *Pranaam*– no path easier than this has ever been heard of! (There was a time) I felt like running up to people and telling them: "Listen! You just do *pranaam*. You will liberate yourself with that alone."

506. All is mine…this is rooted in 'I am the body'. *Namah na mam namah* – one '*m*' *kaar* has disappeared. This body is *na mam* – it's not mine! It is only to forsake this body in the spirit of surrender that you must take recourse to *namo namah*.

507. Progressively as *bhajan* (singing in praise of God) helps build more and more *sattvik* currents in the man's body, he evolves; his mind is turned inwards and he enters the realm of *Anahata Shabda*. Then properly communing with it, by His advice '*Aham-Mam*' i.e. the awareness of 'I-Mine' is at once dispelled. This is to be reckoned as *mukti* (liberation).

508. Say what you like, but all the *Shastras* proclaim that a holy man, sight of the Guru, touch, *pranaam*, service, drinking the water from Guru's feet, eating the remains of the food offered to the deity – all these help grant peace even to the gravest sinners.

509. The place where the holy men and the devotees of God live is surcharged with *sattvik* vibrations in great

concentration. Whoever visits these places experiences the flow; these *sattvik* vibrations enter into their body, waves of joy permeate their being.

510. *Trinadapi sunichen taroriva sahishnuta amanina manaden kirtaniyah sada Harih*[29]. Forever committing the meaning of this *shloka* in one's heart, one must try to act accordingly.

---

29 The devotee of God has to be fully convinced that he (his body) is useless and cheaper than the grass if he is a devotee of Hari.

8

NATURE OF *MANTRA* & *JAPA*

Purpose & Nature

511. *Japa* is the sole expedient for this *yuga*. Drown yourself in God while doing *japa*.

512. There is no simpler way than this. No matter which state you are in, sleeping or awake, standing or sitting, pure or impure, by doing *japa* a human being can achieve perfection. Can there be a better hope than that?

513. Those who are forever engaged in internal or external *japa* are indeed *jivanmuktas*[1] – free of worldly existence.

514. The extent to which a person undertakes *japa* is the extent to which he can be submerged in God. The purpose of *japa* is to increase the divine touch. If you don't forsake *japa*, you will stay submerged in God.

---

1 A full-blown Jnani; a person with full wisdom or a liberated sage. He is released even while living

515. The fruit of a host of spiritual practices is gained through conscientiously pursuing oral *japa* alone.

516. On the foundation of *japa* stands the palace of Brahma *jnana*[2]. If you try to raise the palace of *jnana* without the foundation being strong, you will merely become a hollow prattler of profundities.

517. The purpose of *japa* is to still the mind. If the body keeps moving, how can the mind be still? Therefore doing *japa* while strolling and walking makes the mind still. Similarly, *japa* while sitting still on the *asana* gives joy.

518. As long as there is a stock of evil deeds done earlier, no joy may be derived in *japa*; even so, it is not to be considered futile. Keep doing *japa* whether you derive any pleasure or not – I am sure you will experience the grace of the Divine Mother!

Japa Considerations

519. Why should *japa* be performed on an *asana*? One should not perform *japa* sitting on bare earth because this way it is not possible to make the *mantra siddha* (breathe life into it). Sitting on an *asana* made of blanket helps realize all desires speedily.

2 Divine wisdom

520. All *mantras* spring from Shiva. To utter anything of one's own will or fancy does not make it a *mantra*.

521. If the *Gayatri mantra* comes to your mind as you are chanting *Ishta Mantra*[3], repeat it. Every day you must chant a thousand-count *Gayatri japa*. Regularly observe the *sandhya* worship.

522. If you wish to pass urine or stool during *japa*, go and relieve yourself first and then pursue *japa*.

523. There is no harm in performing *mantra japa* at any time or any place. Ceaselessly engage in *mantra japa*, peace will dance inside you and on the outside; there will not even be a trace of unrest.

Manas Japa

524. Contemplating upon the syllables of the *mantra*, one after the other, and writing them mentally in the heart or in the region of the third eye, and uttering them mentally, is called *manas japa*.

525. The spiritual aspirant must strive to gain a vision of one's favourite deity. Once the vision is obtained – God, in our favoured form, does what He likes.

---

3 *Mantra* of the favourite deity (bestowed by Guru)

Process & Experiences in *Mantra Japa*

526. By tying the rope of *japa* to the pot of the Guru-endowed *mantra* and then dropping it in the well of one's heart, one must draw it up uttering 'Jai Guru'; this can yield excellent spiritual water. It is a way in which human efforts are sure to be crowned with success.

527. As one keeps doing *japa*, the mind is purified. Tendencies of *sattva, rajas* and *tamas*[4] are transcended; trembling, tears, rising hair, *Naad-Jyoti*[5] etc. appear, the soul is filled with joy, and there is tremendous eagerness for vision of God.

528. While doing *mantra-japa* bestowed by one's Guru, when *Naad* and *Jyoti* appear, then the disciple is able to clearly discern 'I am not the body,' one sees the continuity of embodiment, and attachment to the body is dispelled.

529. Women and men of other *varnas* (other than *Brahmins*), will decidedly experience the rise of *shakti* after they complete one lakh *japa* count of *Ishta Gayatri Mantra* at the rate of a thousand *japa* count daily. Those who complete twelve lakh will see fulfillment (of their desires). After that, it is their duty to take up *Naam Samkirtan*, the great *sadhana* of *Kali Yuga*, every day.

---

4 Modes of passion and inertia
5 Divine Sound & effulgence

530. While chanting 'Guru, Guru, Guru' – God's ambassadors appear in the form of *sattvik bhavas* (divine sentiments) – tears, thrilling of the body hair, rapture etc. Thereafter, God appears in the form of *Jyoti* and *Naad*.

531. The *Shastras* state that ten billion varieties of *Naad*[6] and one billion kinds of *Jyoti*[7] play within, either manifestly or unmanifestly. Once the *Naad* is awakened it is sure to drown in *Param-Naad*[8].

532. There are two *Brahmans* to be meditated on — the Sound *Brahman* (in the form of the *Vedas*) and *Para Brahman* (the Supreme *Brahman*). When the devotee becomes accustomed to Sound-*Brahman* (acquires skill in listening to the *naad*-sound), he will attain complete unity with *Para-Brahma Para-Pranava*, that is to say, his consciousness will assume the permanent form 'I am *Brahman*'.

Stillness in *Japa*

533. Even if the mind is not still, it is necessary to do *japa* regularly. Mind is stabilized as one continues to do *japa*. The fruit of *japa* accrues even if the mind is restless.

---

6 Divine Sound
7 Divine Effulgence
8 Supreme sound – *Aum*

534. Those whose mind strays away to other objects while doing *japa* must wear a *tulasi mala*[9] round their neck, wear *tilak* on their forehead and sit in a *tulasi* garden, counting beads of God's Name with the help of a *tulasi mala*, this makes the mind one-pointed speedily and helps develop interest in *Naam*. The *sattvik* sentiment rises, mind enters the inner realms and the person is able to successfully meditate and achieve peace.

535. To be able to count *japa* on the palm is a rare blessedness. Every day, after accomplishing a predetermined count of *japa* sit down with palms joined for as long as you can.

Mantrashesh ~ Consummation of *Mantra* & Realization

536. Standing or sitting, eating or lying down, if one chants 'Ram, Ram' constantly, one will be able to gain His Grace, there is no doubt about it. A person, who is anxious to gain God's Grace, can experiment on this and test its truth. He, who constantly chants 'Ram', 'Ram', will become Ram; he who chants 'Shiva, Shiva', will become Shiva; by chanting 'Durga, Durga', or 'Krishna, Krishna', one becomes Durga or Krishna. This word of the *Shastras* is absolutely true.

---

9 Garland of beads made from the stem of holy Basil

537. When the (inhalatory) breath is in the left nostril, the *kundalini*[10] is asleep. It is regularly awakened when the (exhalatory) breath flows through the right nostril. Special awakening happens through *japa-dhyana* etc.

538. How can one realize the *atma* (Soul)? Guru bestows a *mantra* and doing *japa* of that *mantra* regularly, the *atma* in the shape of Naad and Jyoti, is revealed in the heart. Then the awareness that 'I am the body' is progressively dispelled. *Jiva* is immersed in delight. One is freed from *samsara*.

539. Take the *mantra* to it consummation. When the *mantra* reaches consummation and lapses, *Omkar* manifests automatically. When the *mantra* is consummated, the ability to utter it is lost. As soon as one thinks of the *mantra* the prana enters the *sushumna*[11] through the newly opened channel and unites with *Omkar*.

540. As soon as you have fully realized the *mantra* by chanting it until it is drowned in its original sound body, you will realize you are not a creature imprisoned in the mortal cage and afflicted by disease, sorrow, sins and burning pain. You will realize you have become as unfathomable as the ocean, as vast

---

10 *Kundalini* is described as a sleeping, dormant potential force in human organism. Many term it the serpent power because it lies coiled. It is one of the components of an esoteric description of man's 'subtle body', which consists of *nadis* (energy channels), *chakras* (psychic centres), *prana* (subtle energy), and *bindu* (drops of essence).

11 *Sushumna* is a *Naadi* in the human subtle body. It is one of the body's main energy channels that connect the base *chakra* to the crown *chakra*

as the sky. On your left and right, front and back, above and beneath, happiness is dancing. All around you, in all the ten directions, a wave of delight has risen. You are immersed into the ocean of bliss.

541. No matter what, don't waste the rare human birth! Listen! Sense-gratification is available in the womb of even a dog and a pig, but *mantra* cannot be gained in any other birth. You have received it. *Mananat trayate"*[12] – it is through the mind (*mana*) one is delivered.

542. O Traveller! Do not cry! Put an end to this. Take the *mantra* to its logical conclusion (*mantra shesha*). Just once, try with all your might to merge your *mantra* in its original sound-form. I pledge this under oath – as soon as your *mantra* ceases, you will derive supreme bliss, you are sure to obtain it!

543. Let the *mantra* attain *chaitanya* (be instilled with life), may the (divine) experience dawn; it is then *saguna samadhi*[13] will be possible. The five transcendental objects of the senses will present themselves– transcendental sound, touch, sight, taste and smell. By adopting any one of these you will attain *samadhi*. It is only after this, that all talk of *jnana*[14] is valid. There are several penalties for a fake *jnani*[15]. Be Shiva; don't impersonate Shiva.

---

12 *Mananat trayate iti mantrah* – a *mantra* is that which protects us when we chant it
13 Perfect absorption into form
14 Knowledge of the ultimate reality
15 Knower of ultimate reality

544. The *Shastras* are endless, several are the subjects worthy of knowing, there is limited time and obstacles abound. In this very brief interlude, it is only appropriate for every well-meaning devotee of the Lord to work towards fructification of the *Ishta-Mantra* bestowed by his or her Guru, rather than debating over so many *Shastras*.

545. *Mantra* is peace – take the *mantra* to the culmination point with constant repetition – then you will realize what a great gem Gurudeva has conferred upon you.

546. To bring about *mantra shesha* is to dissolve the *mantra* to its original state; it means *mantra* will come to an end. It will cease to exist. The *mantra* will help you realize God, and cross over birth, death, old age and sickness, and eventually join the joyous ocean of its essential nature.

547. You won't have the power to pronounce the *mantra*. As soon as your mind beholds the *mantra*, your *prana* will internally become still. You will see God; the *mantra* will cease. Leave alone uttering it, at that time you won't even be able to remember *mantra*.

548. I affirm this on pledge, and proclaim it at the top of my voice, if you can take the *mantra* to the point of culmination, repeat it till it's dissolved it in its source (*mantra shesh*); you will attain liberation. You will surely attain it, yes you will!

549. Those who are able to get a glimpse of the Supremely Blissful One, thrice a day (at *sandhya* hours), soon get established in the realm of delight.

How Much *Japa*?

550. Keep doing *japa*; let the days and nights pass one after the other while you have refuge with *Naam*, let your seat of meditation be well established. *Asana jayaat prana jayah*. When you conquer *asana* (stay firm in your prayers in a single spot), you will triumph over *prana* (vital breath) too. Just watch! God Himself will grant you vision thereafter.

551. You have been blessed with this life with Guru's grace. You have received the *mantra*. Put that *mantra* into practice through *japa* and make progress. Be scrupulous in doing *japa* in the morning, mid-day, evening and midnight. *Mantra* is no ordinary thing. *Mantra* is God.

552. It is advisable to do *japa* constantly; it is the bounden duty of a *brahmachari* to make a firm resolve in this matter. Let not the tongue rest without *Naam* even for a moment. Thereafter, the grace of compassionate Lord will descend on him.

553. Many people take *diksha* (initiation) just for the sake of amusement. They give up the required practice in a month or two. What can even a *Siddha Guru* do for

this kind of disciple? It is not fair to do this; if not a full course of a thousand counts; somehow one must do *japa* a hundred and eight times. Effort is a must. How can one expect fruit without any effort?

554. Gurudeva hasn't bestowed *mantra* alone; he has gifted God in the shape of a *mantra*. If you chant that mantra ten or twelve times or a hundred and eight times, how can you gain peace? At least for six months, try and do a *japa* count of 21,600 daily and then see whether you get peace or not.

555. God performs His *leela* by sustaining the human body in the form of 21,600 inhalations and exhalations. Therefore by undertaking 21,600-count *japa* every day, one can reach Him. Whether in one sitting, two sittings, three or four, every day one must perform *japa* for four hours.

556. *Virakta sadhus* (renunciates) should carry out one lakh *japa*-count daily and the householders must achieve a count of 25,000 *Naam japa* every day.

557. The first duty of the spiritual aspirant is to perform minimum of one hour of *japa* thrice daily – at the dawn, noon and dusk. Thereafter, once there is growth of *sattva guna*, sleep will decrease, and it will be possible to get up in the morning after meditating in the midnight.

558. If you can give three-four hours out of the twety-four hours of your day for *japa*, meditation, chanting, reading scriptural texts and other worship, you are sure to get spiritual experiences. You will simultaneously make progress in worldly life. I say this on oath – it's my promise!

Writing *Naam ~ Likhita Japa*

559. Those who can write must write (Ram *Naam*). Depending upon competence, adopt the practice of meditating upon the favourite deity, *sushumna*[16] etc. This will bring you supreme bliss. Basically, only when the *Naad*[17] is gained, *dhyana*[18] is to be practiced.

560. By writing *Naam*, it is possible to quickly get *bindoo darshan*[19]. Utterance of *Naam* may not touch the mind, but writing 'Sri Ram Ram Ram' while saying it puts into action the 'tongue', 'eye' (which is superior organ among the senses), 'mind' (the lord of the senses), and also the 'hand'. It is not possible to *write Naam* without involving the 'body-speech-mind' triad; as a result of this synthesis, abundant *sattvik* vibrations are attracted to the being. It removes the impurities of the body, frees one of disease and bestows *Naad* and *Jyoti*.

---

16 *Sushumna* is a *Naadi* in the human subtle body. It is one of the body's main energy channels that connect the base *chakra* to the crown *chakra*
17 Divine Sound
18 Meditation
19 Vision of the point without a centre from which proceeds the Cosmic Sound (*Naad*).

Ma Japa

561. Blow up the desires, more impenetrable than even the forts made of iron, with the cannon of *Ma Naam*. Lust cannot come anywhere near person who chants 'Ma', 'Ma', 'Ma'.

562. Do not consider yourself happy or sad on account of false joy and sorrow arising from this mortal frame, home, wife and children etc. – call out 'Ma!... Ma!' ... Enter the blissful world of the Mother!

9

DEHATMA BHAVA ~ Body-Consciousness

563. As long as there is 'I' (pride and ego) nothing can be achieved. The root cause of all sufferings pertaining to the outside world lies in the ignorance 'I am the body'.

564. Life after life, human being has gone astray out of sheer ignorance mistaking the 'physical body' to be 'the self'.

565. You are not the body – you have heard this from the *Shastras* and holy men; but you have never tried to experience the truth underlying this. The awareness 'I am the body' – this is ignorance. As long as this body-consciousness is not dispelled, you can't find your Self.

566. The simple way is to chant *Naam* incessantly. The weakness lies in false identification – in the awareness 'I am the body'. Just as a fish lives in water, but the fish and the water are independent entities, an insect

lives in a fig but the insect and fig are separate, similarly, the body and the spirit (*atman*) are distinct from each other – to consider the body to be oneself, this is ignorance-sin-vice (call it what you like).

567. Sin consists in *deha-abhimana*[1], in things like 'I am great' etc.

568. 'If all this is the body of God, then my body is also His.' Reflecting thus, the devotee is filled with joy; he is not scared by the praise of the body, he takes the glory of the body to be glory of God and rejoices in it. As long as he maintains the body, he rejoices in it calling it sporting ground of God. Oh! How wonderful! How delightful!

Aham ~ Ego

569. There are two types of 'I'. One 'I' is false and the other 'I' is true. The false I is the one who says, 'I am the body.' This is ignorance; it is sin and it is the source of all troubles and grief. It is *samasra*. The true I says, 'I am the soul.' The true self experiences, 'I am a servant of God', 'I am just an instrument.'

570. Be free from ego – by no means let the feelings like 'I am great' or 'I am knowledgeable' or 'I am virtuous' etc. , find room in your heart.

---

1 Attachment for the body

571. The purpose of human life is direct vision of God. So keep making progress. Let trivial hatred, violence, the foolishness of 'I am great', 'I am intelligent' etc., go away. Regarding everyone as just another manifestation of your favourite deity, learn to respect everyone in thought, deed and action.

572. Do You hear me? I do not know what is good or what is bad for me, I know that You are doing good to me. I cannot always understand the essence of Your goodness and then I become bewildered. Then I cannot remain exactly Your 'I' and become my 'I', so to say. Make me Thine own – You must, why not?

573. Please bend me on my knees and lower my head. Oh dearest, thus take away my *ahankar* [ego] from me. Make my 'I' yours, so that I may lose 'Myself' and live as yours.

Me & Mine

574. The root cause of the disease of *samsara* lies in 'I', 'myself', 'me' and 'mine'. The degree to which 'me' and 'mine' is pronounced in a man, to the same degree is his misery enhanced.

575. Whatever is happening in this world, whatever has happened, as also whatever will transpire, is the work of he merciful Lord of this universe. He shines forth as the primordial cause, but reflects in the form of

the doer. It is foolish men, devoid of philosophic knowledge, who vainly entertain egoism.

576. No matter who you are, if you develop pride, there is no release for you. Someday that pride is bound to get shattered; you are bound to weep saying, 'Oh! I am nobody, I am helpless!'

577. You will not have to renounce worldly life; you won't have to go into the forest; wherever you are, you still can progress on the spiritual path and be in the world of bliss! The suffering is only because of sense of 'me' and 'mine'.

578. Sorrow exists as long as one feels a sense of 'mine' with regard to *samsara*; the moment one feels 'this *samsara* belongs to God and not me', there can be no trace of sorrow. The life of a householder is in itself a service to Sri Gurudeva. Being fearless with this sentiment and serving Guru (latent in *samsara*) and chanting 'Guru, Guru, Guru', one reaches fulfillment.

579. There is as much suffering, torment and grief as there is 'me-me', 'mine-mine' and masquerading in the external world.

580. The day no bubble or wave of 'I' rises in the heart, that day you can assume Gurudeva has truly assimilated you.

581. What you refer to as 'I,' is the body of Sri Sri Gurudeva. He alone is performing *leela* in this world assuming the form of 'I.' This body is His *leela vigraha*[2]. That is the reason you won't have to perform difficult austerities. Whatever *mantra* you have received, just hold on to it with determination – that will suffice.

582. To look for good living quarters as soon as one reaches a new place, or to assign a good room, house or a spot on the riverbank is also among the ludicrous things of *Kali Yuga*. It increases the awareness of 'I am this body.' Our *Ishta Devata* (favourite deity) takes away this ignorance. 'Everything is my *Ishta*' – how can there be a better house or a better place for me?

583. Now that you have adopted the path of renunciation, don't leave a stamp of 'me' and 'mine' anymore. Listen brother, whichever thing you sign with 'mine', it is going to give you tremendous suffering.

Need for Refuge in View of the False Freedom of Man

584. There is one Being, who is the controller of the whole world; He regulates the sun, moon, stars, planets, all the atoms and molecules in this world to go about their respective tasks.

---

2 God's sporting ground or form in which He plays

585. Nobody is independent, everyone is a doll in God's play, and one has to dance to His tune.

586. We are not free – this is indeed true! Man is not independent; *karmas* performed over several births regulate him.

587. People who wish to stand on their own feet and become great, have to court disaster at every step. But those who take refuge with God become servants and work like instruments. God always protects them.

588. All *sadhana*, *yoga*, worship and sacrifices are meant to firmly realize that we enjoy no free will/ independence. As soon as this knowledge is obtained, the bondage of *karmas* tears away and one becomes truly free and enjoys everlasting bliss.

589. Everyone is bound (by past *karmas*), there is nothing anybody can do, 'I will do this', I won't do this', 'it is better if I do this' – all these are misappropriations of the mind. In reality whatever is to happen has already been determined.

Refuge & *Sharanaagati* ~ Surrender

590. He who takes refuge in Him, surrendering to God with exclusive devotion, can realize Him.

591. 'I am under the influence of the *bhakta* and am dependent (on him). I have no independence' – these are the utterances of Sri *Bhagawan* Himself.

592. He likes to carry the burden
So He appears from Age to Age.
Whoever surrenders at His feet
Saying 'I am yours'
Him He embraces by his bosom
And gives him endless *Ananda*.
He gives him what he does not have
And preserves what he has!
If one can only keep Him in one's mind forever
One can overcome life and death.

593. *Don't suppose this is possible and this is impossible for Me! I can tie an elephant with the lotus-stalk and sink a mountain in the puddle made by a cow's hoof! No one can expect to anticipate the course of my action. Give up worrying about family, wealth, heatlth or unpaid debt. I have done every provision for all your needs. O call me...call me. All your worries shall cease... Fear not! Fear not! Fear not!*

594. Once compassionate Gurudeva has absorbed you in his fold this body belongs to Gurudeva alone. This body is no longer yours – it is Gurudeva's.

595. We are not without support, we have a Being, a kin to protect us, and there is nothing to worry. We have come into this world with scores of *karmas*; we will have to reap their fruits. There is no alternative to repeating 'Ram, Ram' and experiencing it all.

596. That God exists, there is no doubt. Whoever takes shelter with Him has no more fears. 'I have taken refuge at your feet' This is the *Maha-Mantra*; the essence of all *mantras*. Fear not, fear not, son of Amrita[3], God has kept you in His bosom.

597. Sing loudly, *Jai Bhagawan Jai*, Let that song play in air and sky. Has anyone tried to find the sun by lighting lamp? Similarly God exists in this world in every form. He is the *Naami* who is playing about in the form of *Naam*. Sing *Naam* without a pause, and all your troubles will vanish.

598. '*Sharanaagatoham* – I am taking refuge with you'. This is the *mantra* you must keep repeating.

599. 'I have taken refuge in Thee,' always remember this *mahamantra*; with this you will reach the region of divine light, sound and joy. My dear! There is an ocean of delight right inside your heart. Dive deep into it with *Naam* on your lips. The kingdom of peace is near.

---

3 Immortality

600. There seems to be no way other than the *prapatti marg*[4] —the way of surrender, the way of taking refuge in God. My Lord is like a father, affectionate to His devotees. If any one takes refuge with Him once saying, 'I am yours,' no matter what kind of person he is, Lord makes him fearless.

601. 'God is the real doer in this world; we are His servants. Whatever we may do, may it be for His pleasure; let us not undertake any work that will displease God' – those who perform their actions with this sentiment, succeed in gaining eternal bliss on earth.

602. Have you become hopeless? Do not lose heart. Hear me – it happens even now. He who takes refuge in God, gains peace of mind. You may be a sinner, you may be afflicted, you may have thousands of faults; yet you take shelter with God saying 'I have taken refuge with you'. You will certainly be able to gain His *kripa*. It must happen; there is no doubt about it. Hear these words from Bhagawan, 'My *bhakta* never comes to harm'. Be a *bhakta* – you will be relieved of all anxieties.

603. In the beginning there is the pride that, 'I will perform spiritual practices and attain God'. Nobody in this world has the power to lay hold of Him through spiritual practice. It's only when one leaves the entire

---

4 The path of refuge or surrender (to God)

burden on Him saying, 'Now I am powerless, I can't do it', that He comes within one's grasp.

604. When the mind of a person becomes steady through company of saints and observance of duties as prescribed by the scriptures, through the grace of God, it dawns on him, that he is not helpless or without refuge, there is a protector and a provider for him. Then he is not disturbed by happiness and sorrow, peace and unrest, wealth and penury, joy and grief. He is able to clearly comprehend that whatever is happening for his good. Thereafter, he takes recourse to the Name of God and looks at the variegated colours of the material world with great delight, smiling (at its wonders).

605. Thakur (God) is the wealth of the destitute. As long as you call things your own, Thakur (God) keeps away from you. The moment the sense of mine (ownership) completely ends, that very moment Thakur (God) holds you close to his heart.

606. He who has taken up the onus of your life, He will arrange for everything. Why do you want to be burdened with it? Lay the entire burden at Guru's feet saying, 'I surrender. I seek refuge in you!' Having done that, you be fee of all worries. Don't worry about anything. If at all you wish to think, think that you are lying in Mother's lap. Think that the Mother has taken over all your burdens.

607. The only object of a devotees' desire is God. A devotee should take exclusive refuge with God and undertake practices to realize Him. Make sure no other wish in any form finds a place in the heart. 'I have taken shelter with you' – never swerve from this *mantra*.

608. Those who are under my protection, why should they look at sense gratification? My devotees cannot be insects in the excrement of sense-gratification.

609. Renounce worthless concerns and just repeat 'Guru, Guru' while standing and sitting, eating and lying down, keep repeating *'Sharanaagatoham* – I am taking refuge with you,' thereafter what transpires in your favour will be beyond your grasp.

610. *I shall follow the path, along which you lead me*
I shall speak those words which you make me speak.
I shall not take any share of sin or merit
All that is yours, my Lord, all that is yours.

611. How can a human being given to the slavery of the stomach and generative organ, achieve the welfare of the world of embodied beings? You have come to do well to serve this world and to contribute to its welfare. Unless you attain to the state of a *jivanmukta*[5], you won't be able to do good in this world.

---

5 A full-blown Jnani; a person with full wisdom or a liberated sage. He is released even while living

183

612. What appeals to my mind is a sense of servitude. It is better to pray 'grant me devotion' than to pray to Him saying 'liberate me from poverty'. Once you get devotion, there cannot be dearth of anything.

Seek Refuge in God

613. What is the nature of the attraction between the devotee and the Lord? Even as a servant loves his master, a mother loves her son, a woman is devoted to her husband, the Lord is also attracted in the same manner; because, only in these states of emotional transcendence, are the body and the senses absent; what exists is unbounded and infinite love.

614. He who has been arranging food for the baby in the mother's womb for so long, why do you lose faith in that God and become anxious? Don't you do any *japa* or other forms of devotion? If you did, such useless anxiety wouldn't touch you.

615. Submit your mind to *Shastra Bhagawan*[6] with exclusive devotion; He who nourishes the whole world will look after you. You won't need to worry about your food and clothing; you won't have to worry at all.

616. There is water in the Ganges, the trees bear fruit, the earth offers a resting place, there is the cushion of the present; even today alms are offered to a beggar

6 God in the form of the Scriptures

– why do you worry? Your worries are about desires; set them on fire – let them burn off! If you don't set them on fire, you will have to keep on crying.

Worldly Emotions are the Beginning

617. If there were no earthly pleasure in this world (pleasure from the objects of the senses), human beings wouldn't have realized what supremely divine happiness is – it would have been impossible to even imagine it. Sense pleasures therefore bring the delightful news of divine joy.

618. He gives you the vision in material form first, thereafter *brahma-jnana*[7] rises.

Play with God

619. Forget the rest! Just think of playing with God. In the same way as you are pleased while eating, dressing up and sleeping, with the same sentiment live and sport with God, making offerings.

620. To forget you is certain death, I know this all too well. Yet, why do I forget you? Can you, the stealer of my heart, please unfold this mystery to me?

621. *You are the fiddler, we the fiddle*
This is the great truth
Let me never forget this, O my Beloved!
Even in my wildest dreams

---

7 Ultimate (divine) knowledge

622. *You will play your fiddle*
   And you will sing your song,
   whoever will hear, will be enthralled
   And sink he will in your love, O Lord

623. Even talking is a great *sadhana*. The mind is anyway going to chat. It's better to speak to God in that case.

Prema ~ Love

624. God is a love-beggar. Love Him a bit and He will come to your door again and again asking for more.

625. Without *bhakta* there cannot be any *leela* and that is why *Bhagawan* ever longs for a *bhakta*. It is not as if the *bhakta* alone sacrifices all his desires and becomes a frenzied seeker of *Sri Bhagawan*. Even God is overwhelmed by His desire for securing His *bhakta's* presence. Just as the *bhakta* ever beholds the blessed image of his Lord in the emerald-studded mirror of his heart, the Lord also beholds His *bhakta's* image in His own heart and gets completely lost. That is why great men have said that *bhakti, bhakta, Bhagawan* and *Guru*, are all one and the same.

626. One understands immortal love through mortal love. It is only because there is worldly pleasure that the human being seeks supreme bliss and happiness.

627. When a *bhakta*, who has made complete surrender at God's feet, becomes eager and impatient to see him,

gives up everything and is ready to give up his life if he cannot see *Bhagwan*, then God, who is without birth, with the help of his pure *sattva prakriti*, takes the form which the *bhakta* is anxious to see and appears before him. As His body is ethereal, country, time and place cannot obstruct His appearance.

628. A real *bhakta* of *Sri Bhagawan*, who has complete faith in Him, engages himself lovingly in doing constant *bhajan*. He does not want anything in return. He does not care for worldly pleasures or sorrows. He considers even heavenly pleasures to be insignificant. Through his *bhajan* he does not even aspire to attain *moksha* or a face-to-face meeting with God. He does *bhajan* but why he cannot say. But it is a fact that without *bhajan* he cannot stay even for a moment. For him it is impossible to give up *bhajan*, just as one cannot think of giving up one's life for anything because one loves one's life so much.

629. As long as love is tainted with desire, it is worldly love – that love is productive of sorrow; when love becomes desireless, from then on the natural love actually springs. This is the love that brings immortality!

630. Genuine love is desireless. It does not expect anything in return.

631. So long as one does not do *atma darshan* (revelation of his real identity or God in himself), this type of immortal *prema* cannot grow.

632. *Prema* is to constantly awaken the ecstatic devotion which does not tolerate any separation from God. The feeling that 'I am the body', makes a creature forget that he is ever-existent in God in the same way as the rays of the sun remain in the sun, the waves of ocean remain in the ocean, the radiance of the moon is in moon itself. So long as this feeling that 'I am the body' is not removed, *prema* cannot appear.

633. It's possible to stay close to the heart while staying away from the body. The *gopis* did not gain Krishna in union; they found Him in separation.

Ashru ~ Tears

634. Tears are one of the principal offerings in the worship of God. Whoever worships Him with tears, God instantly confers upon him the fruit of worship and makes him peaceful.

635. Nothing purges the heart of its impurities as do tears. The devotee first makes the heart tender with the aqua of tears and then he lays a seat for God in the sanctum of the heart.

636. Cry! Cry to your heart's content! Keep saying, 'Hari-Hari', and shed tears incessantly, drenching your bosom. God loves tears. He becomes a slave to the one who sheds tears chanting His Name.

10

EXTERNAL WORSHIP

637. Despite the fact external worship is not considered high, even those having *bona fide* authority in external worship are not to be found nowadays. You have finely decked up your body, opened shop for your upkeep, you are enjoying yourself in the company of wife and child – you are so immersed in the most mundane pursuits of the external world! Don't you experience discomfort in this situation? How come all the hesitations come up only at the time of daily worship?

638. As long as there is aesthetic attraction and awareness towards external objects, there is need for external worship.

Yathakaal Upasana/Sandhya ~ Wake up in the Morning

639. You will have to try and practice waking up at dawn. Nobody can end the animal propensities in a man who refuses to wake up early morning in the *Brahma muhurta* (pre-dawn).

Importance of *Sandhya*

640. This command of Sitaram is meant for everyone. One must perform *sandhya* and *japa* assuming a seat on the *asana* at prescribed hours. He who has come to realize God, why should he waste valuable time?

641. God is the dearest one for all; He is the most intimate one! That is why it is the duty of man to perform *yathakaal upasana* (timely prayers). In this way one remembers Him uninterruptedly.

642. His first command is, *Aharahah Sandhyanupaasit.* Perform *sandhya* every day, those who desire to realize God genuinely must observe *sandhya* and *upasana*[1] at appropriate time.

643. God's first command is to observe *sandhya. Aharah sandhyaamupaasit.* There was no other *sadhana* available in *Vedic* times other than *sandhya. Sandhya* means *samyak dhyana*, which is an attempt to realize the fact there is One Supreme Being alone who assumes different guises and dwells in this world.

644. Dear traveller! Always keep chanting 'Krishna, Krishna', and do your prayers at appropriate time.

645. If *sadhana* (*japa*, meditation etc.) is done punctually at the appropriate hours, one reaps the result much faster.

---

1 Worship; Upasana literally means 'sitting near' God.

646. Just as partaking of food at appropriate hour aids in releasing gastric juices and digests the food, enhances blood in the body and increases the strength, in the same manner, *sandhya* at appropriate hour helps still the restless mind due the beneficent influence of that hour, and turns it into intellect which can touch the soul and gain supreme bliss. The body-consciousness of 'me' and 'mine' disappears.

647. Three and half thousand crore demons (Mandeha), wage war with the sun in the morning (dawn), at noon and in the evening (dusk), at the time of *sandhya*; the water consecrated through the *Gayatri mantra* and thrown upwards during the three *sandhyas*, quells these demons. Those who do this, obtain the blessings of Lord Sun, for not being outraged by the demons.

God Appears at *Sandhya* Time
648. To neglect performing worship at prescribed hours daily is to renounce Sitaram. To give up praying at prescribed hours is a great sin. *Sri Bhagawan* regularly pays a visit to the devotee's heart during the prescribed hours of worship daily. One must wait for Him daily on the *asana*, if you are not sitting there praying, He comes and returns with a disenchanted mind. Don't let go of this moment of union! Don't miss it! Don't miss it!

649. In the morning (dawn), midday and in the evening (dusk), God appears in the heart of human beings, therefore it is the bounden duty of all men and women to be present much before the aforesaid *sandhya* hours and await His arrival. While waiting for Him, in due course one actually gets His vision, by His grace.

650. You must perform the *sandhya* regularly; make obeisance prayer through the three *sandhyas*, morning, noon and evening. Please tell all my devotees, mothers and fathers, and everyone else that Sitaram seeks the alms of *ananda* (bliss) from everyone. If you pray regularly at *sandhya* hours and try to chant *Naam* constantly, Sitaram will be greatly pleased. I plead with all of you – don't deprive Sitaram of this bliss.

651. Morning (dawn), noon, evening (dusk) and midnight, these four are excellent hours for *sadhana* (spiritual practice). In these hours the *prana* naturally turns towards the *sushumna*[2] current and stabilizes there – it is in this period God descends into the sanctum of one's heart.

652. Those who observe moderation in diet and perform *sandhya upasana* in the morning and night for six months are able to directly perceive *Jyotirmaya Atma*[3].

---

2 *Sushumna* is a *naadi* in the human subtle body – one of the body's main energy channels that connects the base *chakra* to the crown *chakra*
3 Radiant Mass of Self

653. Those who truly wish to obtain a vision of God, it is necessary for them to try their best to perform *japa*, *dhyana* etc. in these four prime times with full devotion.

Neglect of *Sandhya/ Upasana*

654. Those who don't follow the *sandhya* worship at the prescribed hours, in effect show disregard towards God and Sri Gurudeva. They close the gates of their hearts and forbid entry to God and Guru.

655. Dear traveller! Do you really want peace? Do you really crave for God? If yes, undertake *Yathakaal Sandhya*; this is the first command of God. Do not be guilty of violating the first dictate of God. The fruit accruing from *Yathakaal Sandhya* is indeed limitless. Try it out and discover the great bliss which is in store for you?

Exact Time for *Sandhya* or Daily Prayers

656. There is a designated time for every activity. *Sandhya Upasana* too has a designated time. In the mornings, from 24 minutes before sunrise to 24 minutes after sunrise, is the prime duration for morning *sandhya*; at noon, roughly 24 minutes before the sun is overhead and 24 minutes after; in the evening, the principal hour of *sandhya* is 24 minutes before sunset to 24 minutes after sunset.

657. From 4am in the pre-dawn, to 8am, is the first time-slot for spiritual practice. The second time slot begins half an hour before sunset and continues till two hours after sunset. In the afternoon one must try to do *japa* according to what one can.

658. *Yathakaal Upasana* (timely acts of devotion), first of all, provides you the power of the *mantra*; the second advantage comes from the auspiciousness of the time. During these periods *sattvik paramanus* rain down from the sun and the mind is inevitably turned inwards. When one practices sitting at all three *sandhya* periods, there is a rise in the *sattva* quality and sleep is reduced. Then it is possible to sit at night. The three periods are: just before dawn, when the night retreats and the day breaks, at twilight, when the day retreats and night sets in and in the afternoon, 24 minutes before 12 o'clock and 24 minutes after.

Places Detrimental to Prayer

659. It is detrimental to live in places where strong winds blow. *Prana* does not function smoothly in these places, the mind is unable to turn inwards due to the winds; it keeps playing around the body. In places near the seashore and at altitudes in the mountains, powerful winds bring about obstacles in meditation.

Praayaschitta ~ Atonement for Time Transgression

660. The meaning of the term *praayashchitta* is *naitat paapam punah karishyaami* – I shall not commit such

sins again. To perform *sandhya* after expiry of the prescribed time slots is akin to ridiculing God.

Praarthanaa ~ Prayer

661. *Prarthana* (daily prayer) is obligatory for everyone. *Prarthana* is special spiritual practice like *yoga* and *jnana*. It is possible for a person to obtain bliss by practicing just *prarthana* and no other *sadhana*.

662. It is the duty of those who cannot put into effect *prarthana* (daily prayer), to do uninterrupted *Naam japa*. You know, the essence of all these is to keep the mind permanently anchored to Me in one way or the other.

Morning, Afternoon & Evening Rites

663. Rising early in the pre-dawn (*Brahma-muhurta*) and sitting up on the bed, meditate on Sri Gurudeva between the eyebrows and your *Ishta Deva* (favourite deity) in the heart, then do *japa* according to your capacity, go to the washroom after bowing down.

664. Your morning rites could include morning *sandhya*, Guru *puja*, Shiva *puja*, recitation of *stava* and *stotras*[4], other prayers, reading and study of the *Gita*, *Ramayana*, *Bhagavata*, *Chandi* etc. and at least two hours of *japa* followed by a singing *Naam Samkirtan* of *Hare Krishna Hare Krishna Krishna Krishna Hare*

---

4 *Mantras* for ensuring safety and wellbeing

Hare, Hare Ram Hare Ram Ram Ram Hare Hare with *kartaal*[5] for some time. You shall offer *arghya*[6] to Surya, and *pranaams* to Surya, Gurudeva, and *Ishta Deva*, thus accomplishing morning rites.

665. If possible, at noon, perform the mid-day *sandhya*, chant *Gayatri japa* according to your ability, *japa* of *Ishta mantra* and make due offerings in *panch mahayajnas:*
1. *Brahma Yajna* (study of the *Vedas*)
2. *Dev Yajna* (worship of deity and *homa)*
3. *Pitri Yajna (Pitri shraadh tarpan*[7]*)*
4. *Bhuta Yajna*[8] *(Vaishwadevabali)*
5. *Nri Yajna* (worship of a guest).
The guest should be given something. If the guest is residing in the house, the food offered to the deity should be given to him and subsequently had by the host. Do not eat anything that has not been offered to God first.

666. In the evening, after *sandhya* prayers and repetition of *Gayatri japa* according to one's ability, one must sit in *mauna* (silence) at least for five minutes. Thereafter, performing the *mantra japa* according to one's ability, and recitation of *stavas* or *stotras* in the

---

5 Wooden or metallic clapper used in Indian devotional music
6 Water offered to the Lord as a token of respectful greeting
7 Liquid oblation
8 *Bhuta* means all the creatures that have come into existence. Any living being is a *bhuta*. To worship it, to serve it, to see Divinity in everybody, in every creature, is *Bhuta Yajna*.

end, one must sing *Mahamantra kirtan* (*Hare Krishna...*) to the accompaniment of dance. Thereafter, subsequent to having dinner, contemplate Guru in the forehead and *Ishta* in the heart sitting on your bed, and chanting Guru *mantra, Ishta mantra* and *mahamantra*, go to sleep. This will help you attain to your supreme essence.

667. Before eating, one should wash hands, feet and mouth and then with pure food, nourish the body, which is the temple of God. Don't forget: you are not the one who is eating the food; you are serving God who resides within the body.

668. Observing *mauna* (silence) and contemplating upon God, make an oblation to God in the form of *Vaishvanara*. Serving God in this manner with food over a period of time, the vision of Jyortirmaya Atman[9] and His call will be evident to you. Even in the present *yuga* it is necessary to undertake *Brahminical* duties to the extent possible.

9 Radiant mass of Self

11

OBSTACLES TO *SADHANA*
Ahara Shuddhi, Sattvik Ahara, Restraint

The True Nature of Food

669. *Anna* (food) has been referred to as the rope, strength as the peg, body as the abode and *pratyaadhaan* as the head. What do all these indicate?

When, due to the regular eating of *sattvik* food, the *sattvik* strength of the *Prana* is increased, then the *Prana* enters the *Sushumna*[1] and the nine outlets are purified. When the *Prana* is stilled and fixes itself in the *sahasraar*, then the seven enemies referred to before die.

670. Then the root of everything is taking of *sattvik* food?

Yes, *ahaarshuddhau sattvashuddhih*. From eating pure food comes purification of one's self; and from purification of self comes steady intellect. Bhagawan Sri Ramanujacharya has identified this intellect with *bhakti*. When one gains *bhakti* all bonds fall away.

---

1 Sushumna is a naadi in the human subtle body – one of the body's main energy channels that connects the base chakra to the crown chakra

671. Until the diet is purified, the restlessness of the mind does not go away, which is why it is the necessary duty of those who desire health, longevity, strength, and God, to eat *sattvik* food.

672. Food is to be consumed in order to maintain the body. It is the duty of one and all to protect the body through food. Body cannot afford to be weak.

673. *Ahara* basically means grasping of objects (sound, touch, smell etc.) through the sense organs. Once the body is purified with *sattvik* food[2], the organs turn around and the senses are able to grasp sound, touch, taste, sight and smell in the form of God.

674. Food or dietary intake is made up of three parts: one part creates the body, the second creates the mind, and the third part is excreted and discharged. The body, which is created from consuming foods such as meat etc., makes the senses as unrestrained as in an animal; they are directed towards lust and the mind starts singing their tune.

675. The essential substance of the human body is *virya* (virile semen). *Virya* is stuff of soul; to stop suicide imminent through loss of *virya* is rather difficult for those of unrestrained food habits. As a consequence, the body is afflicted with several

---

2 Pure diet

diseases, it is destitute of inner essence and the mind is intoxicated with sense-objects. Then there is no other way than to live in a human body like an animal. Wilful indulgence in *rajasik* and *tamasik* food destroys basic human-ness; the genuine object of one's existence is forgotten.

676. You are feeding Him actually; He is the one who is eating. It is out of ignorance you are pandering to the tongue, killing chicken, fish and egg to fill the stomach. There is no religion in this world greater than non-violence and no irreligion greater than violence.

677. Brahma created rice, barley and gram, so that with these, the human body could be sustained. Goat and other animals were, however, not created for human consumption.

Ahara Shuddhi ~ Purification of Diet

678. By winning over tongue alone, one can conquer all the senses. Just as one takes medicine when one is sick, similarly food must be partaken when one is hungry. Those who wish to realize God must follow this precept in diet.

679. *Ahara Shuddhi* leads to *dhruvasmriti* (permanent memory) and faithful devotion; once this kind of unadulterated and unwavering devotion is gained, the dual knot of matter and spirit in the shape of

the gross, subtle and the causal body is undone. You are set free.

680. The first duty of those who aspire to get rid of the impurities of the body is to eat *sattvik* food and offer worship regularly in the morning and evening. Cleansing the body thus, when the defects of the mind too are dispelled, it is possible to get a vision of the soul in the form of *Jyoti*[3] – there is no doubt about this.

681. When *homa*[4] is performed with pure *ghee*, the aroma of smoke issuing from it purifies the human body and mind. Not only is the man purified, all moveable and immoveable things are purified too.

Food has a Direct Impact on God-Realization

682. If the body is not pure, man cannot experience God. The body becomes pure by observing purity in food and constantly chanting *Naam* (*Hare Krishna Hare Krishna Krishna Krishna Hare Hare, Hare Ram Hare Ram Ram Ram Hare Hare*). Those who partake of *sattvik* food and are of virtuous conduct, they can hear within, the melodious call of God.

683. By serving Him, having recourse to God's Name, and observing pure food habits, His compassion will flow and all sufferings will surely end with it.

---

3 Divine light, effulgence
4 "Fire-offering". A sacred ceremony in which the Gods are offered oblations through the medium of fire in a sanctified fire pit

684. By partaking of impure food and neglecting practices of worship, the substances of the body are despoiled; through *Naam* and pure food, these substances can be transformed and become fit to perceive the Self.

685. When those who eat *rajasik* and *tamasik* food take refuge with *Naam*, they desire not the love of God but worldly happiness, fame, success etc. It is not in the nature of a *premi* (divinely inspired lover) to cause violence. Human beings come into this world to see God; the man who eats *rajasik* and *tamasik* food is unable to recall this even in delusion, he does not have the capacity to understand that he is not the body but the soul.

Effects of Impure Food

686. He who is controlled and eats *rajasik*[5] food can become strong – it is also possible that his mind is sharp; he can discover happiness and general prosperity, but the door of spirituality is closed to him. Sometimes one sees exception to this in a few great souls, but that's a different story.

687. Foods which are extremely bitter (*neem* etc.), extremely hot (tea etc.), extremely pungent (chilly etc.), extremely sharp (pepper etc.), extremely inflammatory (mustard etc.), extremely sour, extremely salty, and those productive of sorrow,

---

5 Rajasik food tastes sour, bitter, salty, has a pungent odour and gives heart and stomach burn. Chilli is a rajasik food.

distress and disease, are all dear to people with *rajasic* tendency.

Anna Nivedan & Bhoga ~ Offering Of Food

688. After food is cooked, it should be offered to God and served with patience and care. He who serves the food must think he is serving God.

689. Whichever caste you belong to, after food is cooked, place a *tulsi* leaf on it and offer it to God saying: 'Thakur (God), please partake of this'. Then, closing the door and standing outside, think that God is partaking of your offering. This done, offer seats to those who are going to eat. Let them wash their hands, feet and mouths and then eat thinking of God.

The Cook: Serving & Attitude

690. It is through this food that the gross body endowed by God is maintained. Therefore, it is important to cook food with great caution, proper procedure, and remembrance of God.

691. Make sure the food is not defiled before it is offered to God; let not even a glance of anyone make it impure.

692. On festive occasions and feasts, before placing the food in the vessels meant for different food items, a *tulsi* leaf should first be offered in the food and only then should the food be transferred to the vessels.

693. Eat *sattvik* food for a few days, have *havishya*[6]. You will notice within a few days of your taking to a *havishya* diet that your body has started becoming free of disease.

694. Those who partake of *havishya* live long and healthy lives, free from disease. They speedily attain God's grace and are worshipped in this world as akin to God.

Fasting

695. The *Shastras* decree eating twice a day; once in the morning, once at night. This affords the fruit of *upavasa* (fasting), which directs the senses inwards. *Tapona-anashanaat parah* – there is no austerity superior to *anashana* (fasting).

696. Everything is dependent on food. God has created man to eat once in the morning and once at night. This way the human being obtains the fruit of *upavasa* (fasting), the mind becomes still speedily.

697. A healthy body is a prerequisite for vision of God. If you have fasted yesterday, it may be difficult for you to do *japa* today, and perhaps impossible to even get up tomorrow. Instead, it is better to take recourse in *mitahara* (moderation in food).

Nature & Power of *Virya* ~ Virile Semen

698. The basic cause is *ananda* (bliss); the foundation of this *ananda* is *virya* (virile semen). When man and

6 Holy food consisting of boiled rice with ghee (clarified butter)

woman unite, the same *virya* is released from the body resulting in tremendous joy.

Restraints

699. Self-restraint is the life of this nation (India). Men and women become immortal through self-restraint. The self-controlled ones remain blissful at their last hour and are ferried across through the *devayana*[7].

700. My dear, it is possible to get direct vision of God through just three expedients – pure diet, virtuous conduct and timely worship.

701. Give up bad company, malicious gossip and addiction of any kind. Always stay pure. *Aacharahinam Na Punanti Vedaah* (even the *Vedas* cannot purify a person of bad conduct).

702. *Kaam, krodha, lobh* – lust, anger and greed are the three open doors to hell. One must forever remain alert with regard to them. Exercise restraint in your speech.

703. In order to walk this path, it is necessary to renounce indiscreet eating habits, evil company and excessive attachment to women. If you cannot renounce these, you will experience hardships and take a long time to reach the goal.

---

7 The path of light, vehicle of light; the path leading to the realm of bright beings. In the Upanishads, it is also called the solar path.

12

SWADHYAYA ~ Self-Study & SHASHTRA PATHAN ~ Reading of Scriptures

Glory of the *Shastras*

704. *Shastra!*[1] I don't know the language which is fitting enough to eulogize Thee, but let me declare it explicitly that I love you dearly. I haven't been fortunate enough to follow all Thy commands, but with whatever I could follow, I have attained my object, I am immersed in the ocean of bliss! I pledge – as long as I am able to utter a single word, I shall proclaim: *Shastra* is true, *Shastra* is firm and resolute; whoever takes refuge with the *Shastra*, God will clasp him close to His heart.

705. My *Shastra* is the vanguard among the host of ways of this country. My *Shastra* is a stream of immortal nectar in the desert of this world. My *Shastra* is the autumn moon shining in the midst of terrible darkness of the new moon night.

---

1 Hindu Scriptural text(s)

706. The path of the *Shastras* is the highway surrounded by guards. Any path other than that of the *Shastras* is a wrong path.

707. God is the protector of the *Shastras*. No power in the world can crush them. Fire is eternally fire; he who tries to kick it will burn his feet.

708. Men and women! Those who read, with devotion, these texts bestowed by Sri Gurudeva, with the intent of assuaging the sorrows of men and women, and giving them happiness in this world, they surely obtain pleasure and delight

Origin of the *Shastras*

709. Who says human beings have written the *Shastras*? Man is surely the recollector of the *Shastras*, but the creator is God alone. God published these scriptures in the hearts of *rishis* absorbed in profound meditation.

Role of the *Shastras*

710. A man takes a dip into the ocean of Brahma with the help of only a single syllable[2]. God stays where the *Shastras* are, their role is to help one determine the truth and be one-pointed with the great unity.

2 Aum

711. Man cannot lift himself up in a single leap; he can gain peace by steadily walking the path of the *Shastras.*

712. It is not easy to gain the fellowship of genuine saints but the holy scriptural texts bestow this.

713. If it were possible to attain everything through *Naam* alone, what is the use of the *Vedas, Upanishads, Samhita, Puranas, Tantra* etc.? Their purpose is to develop loving devotion to *Naam.*

714. As a consequence of sin, human beings suffer many maladies! But these sins too are dispelled by the study of the *Shastras. Swadhyaaya*[3] is among the most powerful ways of doing away with sins.

Nature of & Need for the *Shastras*

715. The *Shastras* are manifestations of Saraswati, the goddess of learning and speech. No one can discern their true import without ascetic practice.

716. One doesn't have to worry about *Naad* (divine sound). It routinely follows one who keeps studying texts and accounts of divine sports of God and sins easily perish, bliss is gained. The destruction of sin awakens a powerful desire to apprehend God, which ultimately leads to God granting His *darshan.*

---

3 *Swadhyaaya* literally means self-study of spiritual quest, achieved through study of scriptures, introspection and holy company

717. The *Shastras* reveal the unknowable; they bestow the formula for happiness on earth. Not only do they reveal the formula, they also indicate the royal way as to how a human being can succeed in obtaining happiness in the world. Which conduct; ethical and social code and custom, should be followed and what kind of rules and policies should be adopted for being blessed with the supreme bliss. This is also described in minute detail in the *Shastras*.

718. To know His identity it is necessary to study the *Shastras*. Who but the *Shastras* will tell us about His true nature? But can the *Shastras*, having emerged out of His breath, succeed in revealing His identity? No, they cannot, except merely providing us with elementary indications.

719. The *Shastras* are here to increase interest in *sadhana* (spiritual practice), not for gaining praise of the people.

720. To flood the mind with religious feeling, it is necessary to read a religious text daily – a book that melts the heart. Sitaram reads divine drama daily; and reading, in its wake, brings great thrill to the body. I derive more pleasure in reading scriptures than in meditation.

721. The texts which contain the divine sports of God are indeed personification of God. By reading scriptural lore, God's grace descends swiftly. By listening to and contemplating these with devotion, human beings win liberation.

Result of Forsaking the *Shastras*

722. Due to the overpowering influence of the *yuga*, the *Shastras* have fallen into neglect. As a consequence of this callousness to the *Shastras*, the world is full of distress. It is the duty of those who thirst after supreme bliss to take refuge in the *Shastras* with exclusive devotion.

723. Forsaking of the path shown by the scriptures has led the people of this country to the present tide of sufferings, torment, disease and sorrow.

724. If one peers into the pages of Indian history, one sees that whenever the demons became powerful, the *Shastras*, *Brahmana* and Mother Cow, were assaulted first. In fact, it was when this oppression grew very strong that God came and re-established *dharma*.

725. The mass of men who have gone astray will not be able to gain peace until they adopt the path prescribed by the *Shastras*, which alone are the streams from which peace can flow.

726. Those who forsake the path of the *Shastras* and adopt self-willed ways, have to suffer from scores of diseases and sorrows.

727. Who can offer peace to those who deride the *Shastras*? It's not possible for them to gain peace... No! It's not possible!

The *Shastras* are True

728. The word of the *Shastras* can never prove to be false. The sea may breach its limits; mount Meru may begin to stir; the sun, moon and planets might deviate from their orbits – these things may happen, but the word of the *Shastras* can never prove to be false. Never!

Security of the *Shastras*

729. The *Shastra*-prescribed path is the secure and well-guarded royal highway. He who walks this path with one-mindedness, reaches the kingdom of that nameless and formless King, with a fearless heart and a smiling face.

730. Listen! The restraint of the *Shastras* is not a restraint; it is the triumphant sound of the drum announcing freedom from attachment. Bind yourself; yes bind yourself with the precepts of the *Shastras*. As you succeed in binding yourself in it, you will obtain more and more bliss. You will surely be happy! This is not something that is hearsay or a bookish fact, it is the great truth concluded from experiences of a long life.

Choosing the *Shastras*

731. Whichever *Naam* you have practiced happily, continue with same *Naam* always. The texts that bring tears to your eyes, bristle your hair, are the ones to be read. Find time to read these. Contemplate on the divine sport of God. This is *Leela Chintan*; it is something you can do even while lying down.

732. In whichever texts are inscribed the name, qualities, divine exploits, tales and divine history of your chosen deity, make these books your regular companions.

733. Whatever you like at a particular time, *japa,* scriptural study or *kirtan*, do just that as per your liking. Everything will add up in your (spiritual) bank balance.

Recommended Texts

734. The devotees of Ram must read the *Ramayana,* devotees of Devi, *Sri Devi Bhagavat*; devotees of Shiva, *Linga Purana, Shiva Purana* etc. – in this way everyone must contemplate, listen to, or sing that text which contains divine descriptions of their *Ishta Deva* (favourite deity). This helps develop one-pointed love in one's own *Ishta*.

735. By studying religious texts like the *Gita, Chandi, Ramayana, Mahabharata, Adhyatma Ramayana, Vishnu Purana* etc., people will derive pleasure. By regularly reading, you gain knowledge therein.

736. Due to differences of religious authority and the devotee's choice, the *svadhyaya* too is different; devotees of Krishna initially undertake the reading of *Srimad Bhagavata*, devotees of Ram, *the Ramayana*, devotees of Devi, the *Devi Gita, Chandi, Bhagavad Gita* and devotees of Shiva, the *Shiva Purana, Shiva Gita* etc. Continue to pursue it until the differences cease, thereafter, whichever text one likes, whichever makes the heart melt, that is worthy of being read.

737. A seeker can read ten principal *shrutis*, one hundred and eight subsidiary *shrutis*, *Vishnu Purana*, and the lives of saints. The human mind craves for newness, which is why so many texts have been composed.

733. The *Mahabharata* is the life of India. Whoever reads it is sure to be blessed. The *Mahabharata* specifically explains the fourfold expedient of *dharma, artha, kaam* and *moksha*[4]. Texts like the *Mahabharata* are best heard from the Guru's lips.

739. The *Srimad Bhagavad Gita* and *Uddhava Gita*, are excellent texts among religious literature. These are beyond compare. I have personally instructed two of my companions whom I hold as dear as my life: 'If anyone can take refuge with these two texts, with these alone, he can attain everything.'

---

4 Dharma or righteousness, Artha or wealth, Kama or sense pleasure and Moksha or freedom through communion with God or the Infinite. These four attainments of life are collectively known as Purushartha

740. By reading the texts extolling the divine sports of one's favourite deity, devotees must contemplate upon that deity as the one endowed with form, formless, gross, subtle and universal. When this contemplation melts the heart and devotional states such as tears, rising of body hair, trembling etc. occur, these will lead to *samadhi*[5].

741. Read *Sri Gita, Sri Vishnu Sahastranaam, Sri Chandi, Sri Maharasayana, Sri Naamamrit Lahari, Sudhar Dhara, Abhay Vaani* etc.

Bhagavad Gita

742. *Sri Gita* is indeed the heart of *Sri Bhagawan*. How much can we understand it? Only by surrendering to Him, He kindly explains it to us; our duty consists in exclusively surrendering to Him.

743. Just as after tasting delicious *amrita*[6], there is no desire to taste anything else, after learning the philosophy of the *Gita*, the seeker after knowledge aspires to know nothing else.

Genuineness of the Shastras

744. The *Shastras*, wherein sense gratification is predominant, are to be reckoned as those where the scripture has been distorted. There is a simple

---

5 State of intense concentration or absorption of consciousness, the product of meditation.
6 Nectar of immortality

benchmark for determining the genuineness of the *Shastras* – that which is based on restraint is genuine and that which does not advocate restraint, is distorted.

745. The fundamental goal of the *Shastras* is final emancipation. The religious statement that has for its end final emancipation, alone can be called authentic. Worldly enjoyments, happiness, gain – this is deformed religious statement.

The *Shastras* & Spiritual Progress

746. The degree to which men hold steadfast to the *Shastras* is the degree to which they can quickly reach the centre of their being. Until man reaches his goal, there is only suffering. By seeking recourse in the *Shastras*, he can easily come out of the grip of sorrow.

747. I offer crores of salutations to the *Shastras* – the bestower of self-knowledge and knowledge of God to the descendants of the Arya race. He who is devoted to the *Shastras* and actively studies them, effortlessly commands *dharma, artha, kaam* and *moksha*[7].

748. The spiritual progress of an individual is directly proportional to his devotion to the *Shastras*.

---

7 *Dharma* or righteousness; *Artha* or wealth; *Kama* or pleasure of the senses; and *Moksha* or freedom through communion with God or the Infinite – these four attainments of life are collectively known as *Purushartha*.

749. Whoever follows the path of the *Shastras* is bound to find peace – there can be no doubt about this!

750. For he who walks the path laid down by the *Shastras*, there can be no obstacle. He is able to win God's favour without much effort. There can be no fall for someone who has adopted the path of *dharma*.

How the *Shastras* Reveal Themselves to the Seeker

751. When anxiety about self-knowledge is awakened, the *Shastra* is revealed. Study of the holy texts produces ascetic inclinations. One realizes, even the happiness derived from wife and children, brings suffering in the end. Reasoning in this manner, one sets out to perform ascetic practices.

752. Unless and until a man devotes himself to ascetic practice and studies, listens to and contemplates upon the *Shastras*, they do not reveal their true import.

753. Ascetics alone are extremely dear to the *Shastras* which impart all their secrets to these people.

754. The *Shastras* and God are not different. Man is able to commit to his heart the meaning of the *Shastras* when he takes to ascetic ways and takes refuge in the *Shastras* with exclusive devotion. It is not possible to obtain peace of mind from shallow and superficial knowledge of the *Shastras*.

755. Religious and philosophical principles cannot be grasped by mere listening or through mental contemplation. As long as the truth behind the words does not directly manifest, that knowledge is just mouthing of words.

Swadhyaaya ~ Study of the Self

756. When there is progress in *svadhyaya*[8], one obtains a vision of one's favourite deity, that is to say, when the mind is controlled and fully concentrated, in forever chanting *japa* of *pranava*[9] or the *Ishta mantra*, or the praise of the favourite deity, progressively as one attains maturity, mastery and an excellent state, the endeavours are crowned with direct realization and vision of God.

757. *Svadhyaya* is an everyday duty like food, sleep etc. Without *svadhyaya* the twice-born ones cannot firmly hold fast to the goal of life.

758. The meaning of *svadhyaya* is to undertake with due understanding *mantra japa*, recitation of *Purush Sukta*, *Vishnu Sukta*, and other *suktas* and *stavas*, as also sing *Hari kirtan*. The practice of studying scriptural texts is also classified as *svadhyaya*.

---

8 *Svadhyaya* literally means self-study or spiritual quest achieved through study of scriptures, introspection and holy company
9 The mystic sound *Aum*

759. *Svadhyaya* incessantly points at the ultimate aim of human life. It helps reach the ultimate goal. With the malevolent effects of the present age, apprenticeship at Guru's residence, study of the *Vedas* etc., is lost. Even now there are a few virtuous men who study the *Gita, Chandi Paath* etc.

760. It is through this *svadhyaaya* that the inertness of the body and tongue is dispelled. The blemishes of the tongue and sins are rid of; there is a surge of *sattvik*[10] sentiment. In every artery and vein, every part of the body, there's a thrill inspired by *svadhyaya*. The body goes into rapture, tears of love roll from the eyes. Due to the uprising of *sattvik bhava*, one is transported into a new world of self-realization.

761. The pleasures of the senses is extremely inferior. He who engages in *svadhyaya* realizes this clearly. *Vaak* is introverted and moves from *vaikhari*[11] to *madhyama*[12], *anahata*[13] sound is heard. In the *veena*[14] of the heart, *anahata naad* resounds on its own. *Svadhyaaya* shows the eternal and fearless path to mankind amd bestows immortality to mortals.

---

10 Sentiments of purity and goodness
11 The fourth and gross stage of *nada* is called *vaikhari*. The spoken sound is *vaikhari*.
12 *Shabda* in its subtle form as existing in the **antahkarana** prior to its gross manifestation
13 Unstruck sound of the cosmos experienced in the *sushumna* channel
14 Popular stringed instrument of south India, often seen in the hands of goddess Saraswati

762. O Men and women, beloved of Sitaram! Teach your sons and daughters to walk on the path of *dharma* right from the childhood. You will be happy if you do so, the children will be happy too, they will succeed in making the most of being born human.

Sri Sri Ramananda *Pariksha Parishad*

763. Sri Sri Thakur has conferred the gems of these books in order to impart knowledge to ignorant men like us. We can read them regularly right from our childhood. It is for this reason he established Sri Sri Ramananda Mahamantra Pariksha Parishad.

764. It is because you love Sitaram and desire the path of happiness; Sitaram is confiding the knowledge of the most excellent path leading to happiness. Through this, boys and girls will be able to build their character, they will acquire the intelligence that's conducive to *dharma*, their courage in virtuous acts will amplify, and they will be free from disease. They will gain *satsanga* (holy fellowship) through sacred books and achieve supreme delight. The children should be moulded right from their childhood.

765. It is the duty of parents to get their children to walk on the path of *dharma*. With this father, mother, sons and daughters can live happily in this world and the next; those parents who inspire their children to walk on the path of *dharma* alone are their genuine parents.

Sanskrit Learning

766. If Sanskrit becomes the national language, by following it, Indians will be able to seek out the way to be inner-directed; they will be able to find the infinite ocean of earthly happiness that lies within the heart of every being. Right from childhood, they will be able to exert themselves towards the goal of human life, which is to realize God.

767. The *chandas*[15] are distinguished into two types – *praakrut*[16] and *vikruta*[17]. The creation of the world proceeds from *vikruta chanda*, the outgoing tendency is responsible for *vikruta chanda*. *Praakruta chand* takes human life to the supreme path of ultimate happiness.

768. Most of the texts written in Sanskrit are bound in genuine harmonious metre; their study enables one to forsake the *vikruta chanda* and move towards *praakruta chanda*. Those who recite *stavas* or *Chandi Paath* etc. loudly, are able to obtain bliss, their body goes into rapture, and hair stands on end, tears flow

---

15 Meters

16 *Praakruta*: etymologically, the original nature/state. Since the original state is 'ultimate happiness', (the union with the Divine/ *Brahman*), the *Praakruta Chanda* refers to those *Chandas*, which take the aspirant back to the original state of ultimate happiness or in modern parlance, centripetal forces.

17 *Viruta*/Vaikruta: etymologically, change or transformation, inferentially, that which is derived from *Prakruti*. Therefore, the *Vikruta Chandas* are the ones which refer to the transformation of the Ultimate Divine (*Brahman*) into the many-faceted world. In modern parlance, centrifugal forces.

from their eyes; even if for a brief span of time, they are surely able to experience supreme detachment. The reason for this is the state of uninhibited release, which is made available to the *pranas*.

769. The study of Sanskrit will effortlessly consolidate our religious existence and achieve the welfare of the world. No good can be done by those bereft of *dharma*.

770. In our country, in the treasure-house of wisdom, how many priceless gems we have! Alas! We haven't had the time to assess them! The *Vedas, Upanishads, Ramayana, Mahabharata, Puranas* and other *Shastras*, have today fallen into contemptuous indifference which has made sorrow, disease, want and sufferings the eternal companions of man.

Books by Sitaram Baba

771 If possible, all of you must read the books written by 'this one'[18] at least once; you will learn a lot from them. They must be read with concentration, it doesn't matter if no tears visit the eye, but thrill is a must; without it, whatever has been read will just flow away.

772. Why have these set of books composed by Sri Sri Thakur manifested? It is because the strength to read the *Ramayana, Mahabharata* etc. is lost. Indulgent

---

18 Thakur Sitaramdas Omkarnath never referred to himself as 'I', he used the term 'this one' or 'this body', to denote his self.

food habits and self-willed conduct has made the mind and *prana* feeble and pathetic, and that is the reason these understandable texts have appeared into this world. By reading these books, the common man will obtain happiness. The Lord has not precluded anyone from the authority of reading these texts.

13

PLEASURE OF THE SENSES – Limitations & Merits

773. There is no happiness in sense-enjoyments; happiness lies in restraint, in renunciation, and it is always established in singing the praise of God.

774. Every object that you find in this material world is restless. For birth after birth, the mind has kept company with these restless things, and is even now doing so, that's why its restlessness shows no sign of calming down; on the contrary, it is constantly increasing. The only restful thing is God and God alone.

775. Consider the Name Ram: for ages, for an eon it has been just the same, immutable, changeless. Keep company with the Name that is still, say *Ram Ram;* all will come aright.

776. God and God's Name are not distinct. Like Him, His Name too is restful and still. Let the mind be in constant contact with God's Name, it is bound to become still.

777. It would be no exaggeration to say that, except the *bhakta* of *Bhagawan*, there is practically no one who can enjoy pleasure in this world without a break for even 24 hours. It sounds rather strange until one probes deeper. It is the mind which enjoys or suffers. One may look outwardly happy, yet be troubled by memories of past life which was drudgery, or overwhelmed by thoughts of the future. Then how is he happy? How can one be happy, who has not the capacity to enjoy pleasure for even one full *danda* (24 minutes), let alone a full day? Only a *bhakta*, absorbed in *Bhagawan*, is always happy. Happiness does not leave him even for one moment.

778. The pleasure that is derived from sound, touch, taste and smell is very little. There is a hundred times more suffering than joy in these.

779. It is only through material pleasure that one can conceive divine bliss. There is a state after which man is capable of experiencing unadulterated bliss at all times. This is the greatest treasure.

Effect of Abuse of the Sense Organs & Body

780. Whichever organ of the body a man abuses, God deprives that individual of the freedom to exert that very organ in the next birth.

781. He who incurs sins with the body, to him God does not grant the bodily freedom in the following birth, which is the reason one is born in the form of a stone or a tree.

782. By sowing the sting of the scorpion, sweetness of sugarcane cannot to be expected; by planting *Babul*, one cannot expect to grow a mango tree. To perpetuate the cycle of creation, it is necessary to properly appropriate God-given organs of the body; to misuse them would mean inviting suffering, a suffering that has to be endured life after life.

783. God deprives the freedom of speech to those who incur sin through speech. Birth in the shape of birds and beasts is the result.

Conquest of *Krodha* ~ Anger

784. Do not insist on satisfying your own will, emphasise God's will instead. You will not be angry then.

785. As long as there is a sense of doership, there will be anger. The cause of anger is opposition to one's desires; for instance, if someone says, 'today I will serve rice and potato curry' and does not really serve it, then there's cause for anger.

786. The easiest way to overcome anger is not to make a *sankalpa* (resolve) to do a thing. From resolution comes

desire, and anger arises when desire is thwarted. 'I wish to go to Rameshwaram, beyond that it's God's will!' This kind of resolve does not produce anger.

787. If you are angry, keep quiet and sing *Naam*. Do not speak as long as anger prevails.

788. When you become angry repeat 'Ram', 'Ram'. Do not speak until the anger has left you. Renounce *rajasik* and *tamasik* food completely. This way, anger will be quickly subdued.

789. Whenever you are angry, look at yourself in the mirror. If there is Ganga or a lake close by, take ten dips or just pour ten mugs of water over your head.

790. We have to repeat *Naam* when overcome by lust or anger. These will flee as *Naam* is repeated. They will surely disappear.

791. Always keep yourself busy with some work. If an impulse of anger or lust appears, sing *Naam* loudly until the agitation subsides. Do not stay without *Naam* even for a moment.

792. Lust and anger are the enemies of the spiritual path. These are to be conquered with the help of the *Agneya Astra* (fire missile) in the shape of *Naam* and the sword of contemplation.

Overcoming *Kaam* ~ Lust & Restraint in Conjugal Life
Kaam ~ Lust & Overcoming It

793. Of all the things difficult to overcome, *Kaam* (lust) is the greatest foe. Though it is is hard to surmount, it can still be won over.

794. Desire is akin to Raktabija[1]. How can one destroy it? Well, a person who chants *Naam* all the time does not even realize when and where all desires have fled. All desires tender a fearful salutation and runs away from him who takes refuge in *Naam* chanting.

795. Let no one consider himself above sexual attraction or immune to its harm; as long as one is alive, both men and women must be on guard and protect themselves from lust.

796. He who gets a crore of gold coins, will he desire a penny? In the same manner, he who has tasted inner bliss, will he crave for inferior carnal pleasure? He who has scaled great heights and is established on high, low-grade pleasures of this world cannot reach there.

797. Like taste, which is destroyed on having ulcers, you are repeatedly drawn to sexual pleasure and away from

---

1 Raktabija (literally blood-seed), the demon mentioned in *Chandi*, was an almost invincible evil force. If attacked with a weapon, from every drop of his blood sprung other clones of this demon. The Divine Mother Kali rolled out her huge tongue and swallowed all of the Raktabija clones.

your great essential nature; (it's a pity!) you have started declaring yourself to be ordinary creature.

798. Today you are fallen because of extensively mixing with sensualists. You have forgotten the adage *putraarthe labhate bhaaryaa*[2]. You are procreating with strength gained from eating unnatural foods. You are not even limiting the production of children. Think about it! Give it some thought!

799. Unfortunate *brahmacharis* who laugh and make merry with women cannot be saved by anyone in the world.

Adultery

800. Of all the sins in this world there is none equal to illegitimate association with another's wife.

801. Every woman other than your wife is *Jaganmata* (World-mother); always bear that in mind. Make no mistake about this. Can you imagine the suffering (in violating this)?

Reason for Attraction Between the Sexes

802. There is just one reason behind this attraction between man and woman. This world came into being through the union of Purusha and Prakriti. There is no object in this world that is not composed of these two, and this is the reason they attract each other.

---

2 Wife is obtained for the sake of the son

803. What is the attraction between man and woman? It exists because creation is made with both man and woman. It's like a single brick which you can see, which is *prakriti*[3]; what you are unable to see is the one who holds the brick, he is *Purusha*[4]. That's the reason there is attraction. What is seen is *Prakriti* – that which cannot be seen is *Purusha*.

Restraint in Conjugal Life

804. Are your children genuine and natural? It is impossible to have a virtuous child without austerity accumulated by parents over several lives; it is nothing extraordinary to give birth to sheep though! Investigate this – many children are rebelling against their parents; as for those who are of a virtuous turn, you are unable to show them the path. How can you? You are yourself unaware of it; you have been burning all your life in greed for money and pondering over lust. How can you teach them anything?

Paap Kshaya ~ Destruction of Sins

805. No matter how clandestinely and secretly a person sins, the sun, moon, fire, and the firmament; day, night and twilight; earth, water and wind; and *dharma* Himself, are always witness to sin. Chitragupta writes down sins accumulated over several lives in his ledger and metes out retribution over many lives. In that life in which a

---

3 Primordial Nature, which in association with *Purusha*, creates the universe
4 The eternal Conscious Principle of *Samkhya* philosophy – the Absolute.

person has exclusive refuge in God's Name, Yamaraj personally erases all the sins from the records and sets the person free.

806. How will you know whether *paap kshaya* (destruction of sins) is underway? You will begin to develop interest in *Naam*, you will develop devotion towards parents, and you will begin to like religious texts. (These are the signs testifying to destruction of sins.)

807. The sinner can rid himself of his sins by confessing to people, repentance, undertaking ascetic practice, study of religious texts etc. Even reading of the *Gita, Chandi, Ramayana* etc. can deliver a man from sin. He obtains the desired object; knowledge arises in him.

808. A sinful person can undergo penitence as per the *Shastras* and undertake regular *japa*. This will lead him to the companions of God's heart viz. *Naad* and *Jyoti*, divine touch, taste, smell etc. These in turn will lead him to God.

809. Progressively, as the physical body is purified and the mind is internalized, material aspirations are reduced.

810. The flame of a lamp does not flicker left or right, it directly rises upwards. If you try to curb it under a lid, the lid will be blackened with soot. In the same manner, the flame of the soul is forever directed

upwards. Past *karmas* put a lid on it and tarnish this body with various sins.

811. The root cause of all sufferings is sin. Through virtuous deeds, visiting holy places *(titrthas)* and rendering service to humanity, one is divested of sin and gains the company of *sadhus* and interest in *dharma*. Desire to listen to tales of God follows.

812. Great is the power of God's *Naam* and *Katha* (divine history)! When His Name and qualities are heard, He appears in the heart and rids one of evil desires. There is no purification greater than *Naam* (divine name), *Leela* (divine sport) and *Guna* (divine qualities).

813. The cause of disease is evil doings. These deeds may not have been committed in this life, but how can their fruit be lost? Misdeeds of earlier births present themselves in the form of disease to relieve devout men of their sins.

Fall from Spirituality

814. If gold is thrown into the mud, it does not become iron, but it is smeared with dirt. In the same way, he who has seen God does not suffer a downfall, but his body can be tainted with dirt. Therefore, even the God-seer must be on the guard. It is their duty to go only in that direction in which there is no danger of falling from the ideal.

815. Due to the influence of providence, if a *sadhu* does an evil deed, he must confess it in front of others without hesitation – this does not bind him in attachment to the deed. A person embarking upon fresh *karmas* is sure to fall from his spiritual practice if he keeps his sin secret and remains attached to it.

816. When virtuous and evil deeds are both absent, there is no possibility of assuming a human body. When the minds of the lower rung of devotees lustfully go to another's wife, due to influence of sinful *karmas*, through the grace of God that attachment is dispelled. The mind of the excellent and the medium rungs of devotees are not attracted towards another's woman.

817. If practices such as *karma, yoga, jnana, tapasya* etc. are undertaken without taking refuge with God, there is a great possibility of a fall. God always protects him who has taken refuge with Him.

818. Until such time that the spiritual aspirant does not obtain vision of the favourite deity, his fall is definite. But after the vision, if one imparts *mantra* by God's command, with the welfare of all beings in mind, those bestowals do not result in his fall.

Patan ~ Fall

819. Like a flower that is exalted in its fall, enthusiasm increases after the fall. Suppose, you set out to take a holy dip in the Ganges, and some obstacle crops up *en route*. You could even die on the way, but the fact remains that you started with the purpose of taking a holy dip. Take another example: One is going to Badrinarayan, one has to cross ups and downs *en route*. While going down he is not visible, but once you have come down, you can surely behold him as you ascend.

820. Sometimes one falls during the course of spiritual practice. How does one figure out whether it is a fall or something providential? How is one to know if it is *prarabddha*[5]? If some bad deed is done, but after that it is confessed to everyone or atoned for, this is *prarabddha*. If this does not take place, and one gets drowned in it, one can take it that it's a new *karma*.

821. Those who are held in favour by Guru, even if they perform wrong deeds and stray away from the Guru *mantra* etc., Guru does not forsake them.

---

5 *Karma* nearing fruition

14

RESTRAINT

822. It is better for all peace loving men and women to keep away from saints who approve of desire-driven or indiscrete lifestyles.

823. How long can an unrestrained person of willful conduct remain energetic? Five to seven years at the most! Thereafter everything is gone. The body gives way; one loses both physical and mental health.

824. Just think! Those who haven't done good deeds – those who have done exactly what they pleased, regardless of good and evil, how can they see God?

825. If all the senses are not held in control and allowed to function in an unrestrained manner, it amounts to misusing them; the consequences are inevitable.

Tongue ~ Conquering Speech

826. The tongue is the foremost of all the senses; it is easy to conquer the other senses once the tongue is won

over. The way to conquering the tongue is to repeat 'Ram Ram' always.

827. In the spiritual world one has to conquer the tongue first. It is not possible to conquer any other sense organ without being able to win over the tongue. The tongue ardently longs to relish *shadrasas*: the six flavours (bitter, astringent, sweet, pungent, salty, sour). It is the duty of the seeker to renounce these flavours in every possible way.

828. You'll have to control your tongue. Garrulousness, talking excessively results in depleting one's power. The degree to which the inner power is littered through excessive talking, to that degree a person will be rid of *sattva*[1].

829. You are not dumb, you have the gift of a tongue, but by talking ill of others and indulgence in eating, the tongue has been defiled. By singing *Naam* and His attributes, always purify it – may the tongue be purified!

830. Oh tongue, the great discriminator of all tastes, you always like sweet tastes. Oh tongue, be pleased always to drink the *amrita*, whose name is Narayana. The ordinary sweet taste of sugarcane, honey etc. end, but the *amrita* of Narayana *Naam* is endless, limitless, and measureless and you will never be able to finish it.

---

1 positive moral, ethical and spiritual power of righteousness and truth

831. Control your speech. Without control of speech, peace cannot be obtained.

Overcoming Defects

832. Lust, anger, *nishwas* (breathing in), fear and sleep are the five defects of the body, the *dosha panchaka*. These are dispelled through *nissankalpa* (absence of resolve), *kshama* (forgiveness), *laghu ahara* (light and moderate meals), *apramaadata* (mindfulness) and *tattvaseva* (impersonal objectivity about truth). Lust is dispelled by absence of resolve, anger through forgiveness, *nishwas* through moderation in food, fear through *manoyoga* (effective absolving the mind) and sleep through *tattva vichara*.[2]

833. My dear, do you really care about your own welfare? Do you really want to make the most of having assumed the human form? Has that desire (for perfection) really awakened in you? If yes, you must renounce six defects: excessive sleep, indolence, fears that keep you from acquiring sound character, anger, laziness, *dirghsutrata* (procrastination due to disinterest) and *chirakriyata* (postponing things, 'I will do it', 'I will do it').

---

2 Note: Patanjali (1:30-44) Discusses the obstacles *chittvikshepaah* in the spiritual progress of the aspirant. In 1:34, he lists those thoughts and actions, which result in pain where he includes anger (*krodhah*), greed (*lobhah*), and violence (*himsaa*).

834. Some people say we have seen someone who chants God's Name continuously yet commit bad deeds. These people don't understand that the good or bad deeds a man performs are often inspired by the impressions of a previous life. It is possible that through tendencies of a past birth, a person who chants *Naam* (or a generally religious person), might commit some offence, but if this be the case, his present attempts at chanting *Naam*, which result from supremely virtuous deeds of a past life, are bound to be successful. Can they ever be wasted? No, that cannot be. God destroys all the sins of a person who chants *Naam*.

Mauna

835. This world was created out of *vaak*, the articulate word, therefore those desirous of walking on the spiritual path and attaining peace, must observe *mauna* for a predetermined duration daily; one can undertake two or three hours *mauna* in the morning for instance.

Concentrate On One Thing

836. By resorting to one path everything is realized. By taking to many paths everything is lost. First of all one must get *diksha* (initiation) and try with all one's might to attain *mantra siddhi*[3]. By practicing as per the prescribed tradition, the *mantra* is sure to turn *siddha* (realized).

---

3 When the *mantrashakti* is awakened by *sadhana*, the presiding *Devata* appears, and when perfect *mantra-siddhi* is acquired

837. There is no point in reviewing too many scriptural texts. Adopt the *bija mantra* bestowed by Gurudeva, and read those texts that are conducive to it.

Seclusion & Solitude

838. In order to make progress, it is necessary for everyone to meditate regularly and perform austerity in a secluded spot. This brings about the welfare of the world. Without solitude man cannot achieve perfection.

839. There is no escape from agony if you stay intoxicated with the sense-objects. I am very fond of solitary, uninhabited places. Go, chant *Naam* sitting in solitude, and I too will sit there and listen to it. Do not contest the fact you are not able to see me. I am merely waiting for the right time; the moment the time is ripe, I will appear before you.

15

THE BRAHMIN

840. If a Brahmin undertakes a *Gayatri japa* count of one-thousand every day, he will achieve a total of one lakh *Gayatri japa* in three months and ten days; continuing at this rate, he will complete twelve lakh count of *Gayatri japa* in three years and four months, with this he will acquire full *brahminhood* and reclaim all the lost (spiritual) vigour.

841. Offer prayers at the appropriate hour every day. It is the bounden duty of every Brahmin to do *trisandhya*[1] daily. Other castes should only do *japa*, meditation and prayer.

842. Purify yourself through penance, observe *sandhya* thrice and do a thousand counts of *Gayatri japa* daily – then God will not stay far from you.

---

1 *Tri* means three. *Sandhya* means a juncture of time of a day. The word means the ritual speaking of the *Gayatri Mantra* by a Brahmin three times a day, morning, noon and evening

843. O Brahmins, venerable among people! You come into this world to impart knowledge to men. Shine once again, with your practice of truthfulness, virtuous conduct, renunciation and austerity!

844. It is the necessary duty of a Brahmins to observe *sandhya* at the three prescribed hours. A Brahmin who shirks from religious duty, is self-centered and intent on worldly comforts, he is indeed fallen. He should observe restraint and *brahmacharya*.[2] He must eat *sattvik* food and every day complete a hundred and eight counts of *Ishta Gayatri japa* and one thousand and eight counts of *Vedic Gayatri japa* with the intent of gaining the grace of *Ishta Deva*. It is after he has completed one lakh count of *Gayatri japa* that he will clearly realize that there is an awakening of energy within him.

Brahmacharya

845. The body cannot remain healthy without celibacy; through the unbounded power of *brahmacharya*, even a human being can become God of the gods.

846. Those who are able to maintain *brahmacharya*, things work in their favour and turns every piece of their food into pistachio, raisins, milk, *ghee* etc.

---

2 He who has congress with his wife only once in the prescribed period is also considered a *Brahmachari*

847. Come, you immoral one! See what state this country has come to, due to meaningless destruction of *virya* (virile semen). You know what it is in your heart. Even now there is hope. *Sattvik Ahara, Yathakaal Upasana* (21,600 count of *Ishta mantra japa*) and *brahmacharya* (celibacy) – observe this and study religious texts. You will be able to acquire God's grace, your lost *virya* will be restored, and you will gain a new lease of life.

848. The root cause of good health is *brahmacharya* (restraining carnal desire). If you don't observe *brahmacharya*, it is meaningless to talk of the body, *dharma* or knowledge! There can be no pleasure without *brahmacharya*. There can only be lifelong tears!

849. Without the observance of *brahmacharya* (holding of one's semen within by abstaining from wasting it through sexual activities), a man cannot gain genuine human character. Onion and other extremely aggravating foods (productive of negative tendencies), not in keeping with the *Shastras*; reading sensational dramas, novels; and non-observance of *shaucha*[3] rites, hinder the mind from moving towards God. Thoughts about women vehemently rush to the mind.

---

3 Observance of internal and external purity

850. The river of consciousness is flowing in both the directions – it is flowing towards sin, and towards well-being as well. If you don't let her course on the righteous path of well-being, she will surely drift along the path of sin. She won't stay still. He, who spends time in the company of women or thinking about them, cannot observe *brahmacharya*. An individual without *brahmacharya* has no strength of the mind.

851. The phase of long adolescence of your life is on its way. If you don't practice *brahmacharya* and restraint now, you will be carried away in the strong currents of youth. You will not be able to enjoy (material pleasures) for a long time – you will have to suffer from chronic diseases and lament throughout your life.

852. Sitaram proclaims to all the students, men and women, 'How many books have you all read? How many exams have you passed? Sure, you have received much happiness and merit from them – but regular study of the *Gita, Chandi,* and *Ramayana* etc. can offer you benefit many times more pronounced than that. You surely stand to gain a lot more'.

853. To maintain *brahmacharya*, physical exercise is extremely conducive. Everyone must perform physical exercises.

854. Actively work towards maintaining strict *brahmacharya*; eat *sattvik* food! You are trying to strengthen your body by forcibly eating eggs, meat, onion etc. Hari! Hari! How can you ever achieve health with that?

855. This is what I wish! I wish to initiate the young into the *brahmacharya vrata*[4]. Yes, you have enjoyed the company of women enough! Now forsake the company of woman and see what happens. I will grant you more happiness.

Advice to the *Grahasta* ~ Householders

856. You have created your *samsara* with your wife, children and relations; that has become the centre of your world. You have no idea of anything outside of it.

857. Your wife, son, daughter, son-in-law and your self – this is your world; with your ability to feed these limited individuals, do you think you have achieved the ultimate? No! No! You are not so small. The entire power of God lies within you.

858. It is the duty of every *grahastha* (householder) to render services unto *atithis* (guests), for the *atithi* is Narayana incarnate. No matter what means you have at your disposal, a meal, a single *roti* or a sweetmeat, a single paisa, the guest should be worshipped with such offering.

---

4 Vow of continence

859. Don't let young boys and girls eat eggs, meat, onion, tea and other negatively stimulating substances. Arrange to get milk or good quality *ghee* for their nutrition. Those who nourish their children with improper diet will regret it in the long run; even sweets should be served in limited quantities.

860. If your parents are alive, serve them as if they were gods. Worship them with flowers, drink the water after washing their feet and be obedient to their commands. Serve other elders according to your ability.

861. It is an essential duty to perform *shraadh* (last rites for the departed souls) and *tarpan* (offering water to them), to serve God and the cows, to do your daily worship at the designated hours and always stay yoked to *Naam*.

862. Those who are in service should complete their morning and mid-day *japas* at one go. Once at the workplace, start work after praying, 'God, give me strength'. At the end of the working hours, salute Him saying, 'God, please take the fruit of my work', return home and do *japa*, meditation and prayer according to your capacity.

863. As far as possible, do *satsanga* (be in the company of holy persons). Always try to chant *Naam*. Either alone or with co-devotees, chant *Tarak Brahma Naam Sankirtan* for a while every day.

Trividh Rina ~ Threefold Debt

864. A human being comes into this world overwhelmed by three kinds of debt. *Deva rina, rishi rina* and *pitri rina* (debt to deities, sages and ancestors). The debt to deities is repaid through *puja* etc., the debt to *rishis* is repaid through study of the *Vedas* and other *Shastras*, and the debt to *pitri* is repaid by giving birth to a child.

Atithi ~ Guest

865. When guests come home, receive them lovingly and serve them as much as you can, with due hospitality. Even when you give alms to the beggars, try to bear this spirit in mind that you are offering it to God.

Who is a *Pita* ~ Father?

866. Listen! He who fills the mother's breast with milk for the unborn child has made provisions for food. Those who focus on Him and not merely on food, those who inspire their children towards God, they alone are worthy of being called *Pita* in the true sense.

Responsible Parenting/ Family Life/ Marriage

867. Whether it is a man or a woman, everyone has assumed this human body in order to obtain sight of God. Parents who exhort their children to work towards God-realization are the only parents in the true sense.

868. You have got a professional degree and done your post-graduation. You earn a lot. How much more money will you earn? With whatever money you have, serve your parents. Undertake to do virtuous acts. Take a wife with the feeling that these are two bodies but one soul – walk the path where love floods. Let your human life attain blessedness.

869. Everyone is educated these days, earning money and hving status, but where is the satisfaction? The root is lost somewhere. That's why I say discipline the *prana* and reclaim the lost strength.

870. Watch over children and younger siblings. Ensure they do not fall into bad company... Give them good books. Ensure they observe rites of purity and perform *japa* twice a day.

871. Keep an eye on your children. If they have been addicted to bad habits, help them desist from the same. Do not allow them to fall into bad company.

Duties of *Brahmachari*

872. All the sinful and virtuous deeds of men are stored in the orb of the sun[5]; God offers these to human beings at the appropriate time.

---

5 These are stored in the form of subtle impressions or akashic records

873. Be obedient to the authority of parents and Guru; offer them *pranaam* thrice a day. The blessings of parents and dust from the Guru's feet, improves the lifespan, the body stays healthy; intelligence is enhanced. Show deference to holy men.

874. Human beings have come into the world to obtain *darshan* (vision) of God, and must perform *sandhya* and morning and evening *japa* every day from childhood. It is the duty of Brahmin boys to observe three *sandhyas* and do a thousand counts of *Gayatri japa*.

875. You will win the world if you can manage to keep 'Ram, Ram' on your tongue always.

876. You should concentrate on studies; do not read bad drama and novels, do not associate with boys and girls who are accustomed to vice and improper conduct.

877. Work hard, always be engaged in work. Sorrow is a regular companion of indolent ones.

Serving One's Mother & Father

878. He who is devoted to his mother and father can rise to impossible spiritual heights. He doesn't have to perform any other spiritual practice in order to realize God. God grants him vision of his own accord.

879. The son who serves his mother and father with devotion is surely the master of the world. In Pandharpur, Maharashtra, God voluntarily gave *darshan* to Pundarik, the devout servant of his mother and father, without any solicitation.

880. Remember that human birth is meant for obtaining vision of God and carry on saying 'Ram Ram'. Offer *pranaam* to your mother and worship her. (Touch) your mother's feet; it will result in increase of longevity, strength and intelligence.

881. The son who doesn't serve his father and mother, who misbehaves with them, addresses harsh words to them, refuses to look after them and give them food, for such an unfortunate son, even great religious duties prove fruitless. The son who hates his mother and father has to suffer torment in hell for an infinite length of time.

882. There is no remedy indicated in the *Shastras* to check the advance to hell of a son who is hostile towards his mother and father. He suffers hell while he lives, and after his death too, he continues to suffer it for an infinite length of time.

General Duties

883. It is the duty of a Brahmana to observe three *sandhyas* daily; the duty of a son is to serve his parents as though they were the mother and father of the whole world;

the duty of a wife is to serve Narayana in the form of her husband. It is everyone's duty to forsake prohibited foods, have food and water only after offering it to God and constantly chant *Naam*.

Advise to *Sadhus* ~ Renunciates

884. Leaving one's bed in the *brahma-muhurta* (pre-dawn), contemplate Sri Gurudeva in the head and *Ishta Deva* in the heart, then mentally offering worship, offer salutation to the earth and proceed for daily ablutions.

885. It is the duty of a *brahmachari* to bathe thrice a day. Separate quarters should be maintained for *japa* etc.; thrice should God be worshipped, and if it is possible, *nityahoma*[6] should be performed with one hundred and eight *Bilva*[7] leaves.

886. A pure, frugal and *sattvik* diet is to be had twice, in the morning and at night. It is your duty to read the *Gita*, *Chandi*, *Srimad Bhagavata*, and *Ramayana* etc. *Naam Sankirtan*, *Ajapa-Japa*[8], *Gayatri* and *Ishta Mantra Japa* are to be done regularly.

887. Brahmins should perform *sandhya* at the prescribed hours every day and also worship and prayers, *japa*, meditation etc.; members of other orders must take

---

6 Daily fire sacrifices to the Lord
7 A sacred, wood apple tree, associated with Lord Shiva
8 *Hang-Sah* – the *mantra* of inhaling and exhaling

to scriptural reading, chanting, meditation etc. It is necessary to do *asana shuddhi*[9] (this is stated in *Guru Gita*).

888. Do *japa* and *dhyana* thrice, rising early in the pre-dawn (*brahma-muhurta*), mid-day and evening, and (if possible), also at midnight.

889. *Leela chintan* (contemplation of His divine sport), contemplation on Guru (favourite deity), Guru and on *Naad* (latter in the case of those who have experienced the *anahata naad*), are duties.

890. Eat *sattvik* food. If the tongue craves for pungent or bitter dishes, overcome it by starving it with the barest minimum of it. By eating only twice a day, in the morning and night, the merit of fasting accrues.

891. Make an offering of *Vaishwadeva Bali*[10]; offer whatever you eat according to the rite prescribed in the text *Sri Vaishnavamatabja Bhaskar*. If it is not possible for you to observe the *ekadashi* [11]fast, eat only fruit and drink water once. Observe vows on auspicious days like *Janmashtami*[12].

---

9 Purification of the seat, posture
10 Recognition of human dependence on animals and also one's duty towards the poor and helpless. It consists of giving food to as many of them as possible.
11 Eleventh day of every fortnight, wherein fasting is prescribed by the scriptures
12 The auspicious day of the birth of Lord Krishna

892. Do not sleep during the day. Pursue *satsanga*[13] or read religious texts.

893. Eschew evil company. Do not read sensational dramas, novels and cheap literature.

894. Special attention should be given to timely prayers. Prayers should be offered thrice every day. Being prayerful always, one must practice holding a dialogue with God.

895. Every day undertake to read, study *Sri Gita, Sri Vishnusahastranaam, Sri Chandi, Sri Maharasayana, Sri Naamamrit Lahiri, Sri Abhayvaani, Sudhadhara* etc. and if possible, recite the *Srimad Bhagavata, Sri Ramayana* etc.

896. Do not enter a householder's abode with any ulterior motive.

897. Accumulation is good for a *grihastha* (householder) but not good for the devotee of God. May you be among the exclusive devotees of God!

---

13 Company of holy men and the virtuous ones

16

THE MIND

Mind, the Creator of *Samsara*

898. The object of all *yogas* – *Mantra, Hatha, Laya* etc. is to obliterate the mind which is the creator of *samsara*[1].

899. God has laid out the deluding mirage in this world through the mind; as long as the mind exists there can be no *mukti*.

900. *Buddhi* (intellect) is per se a steady principle, when deformed, it results in unsteadiness of the sense organs. When *buddhi* (intellect) is clouded by desire, it is known as *mana* (mind).

901. Conversely, when *mana* (mind) is rid of *rajas* and *tamas* qualities and becomes steady and firm, it no longer remains the mind; it assumes the status of *buddhi* (intellect). Mind is nothing but a name for an unsteady intellect.

---

1 Phenomenal world

Purification & Stabilizing of the Mind

902. The purpose of human life is to realize God. The *Gita* states that without purifying the *chitta* (mind), it is impossible to realize God and gain the knowledge that 'everything is God'. *Nishkaam Karma*[2] is aimed at purifying the *chitta* (mind).

903. Are you saying you cannot still the mind? How can it be stabilized? Have you ever tried to still the mind? If not, how can you expect to still it at once?

904. For a long time you whipped the mind to go after sounds, tastes, forms, touches and smells. You have eaten everything indiscriminately, kept the company of all kinds of people. You never observed any restraint of thought or conduct, never called out to God; this is the reason your mind is not able to calm down.

905. The ways to stabilize the mind are – *ahara shuddhi*[3], living in a pure mental state, and singing *Naam* always, while standing, sitting, eating or lying down. Undertake *vaachik japa* (oral) first, then the *upaanshu japa* (audible only to one's own ears) and finally *manas japa* (mental); once initiation in genuine *japa* is made, one does not have to wait too long to still the mind.

---

2 Working without expectation and surrendering the fruits of action to God
3 Scientific purification of diet

906. Sitting on the banks of the Ganga, stare at the water for 30-45 minutes, continue to look at the water – your mind will very quickly become one-pointed.

Mind Control

907. O mind! 'I will first make my mind free of worries and then set out to perform spiritual practice' – don't harbour such illusions. Commence right away! As long as you are embodied, there will never be a time when your worries will end.

908. The reason for restlessness of the mind is *rajoguna*. By taking recourse to *satsang*, reading of scriptural texts, eating *sattvik* food and drinking Tulsi juice, the *sattva* is enhanced and the mind is stabilized.

909. The very purpose of *sadhana* is to conquer *laya* and *vikshepa*[4]. During the course of one's spiritual practice, the mind is bound to be restless. *Siddha avastha* (perfection) is the ability to dwell in a state of oneness.

910. Many people say that their mind is unstable, that *japa* does not succeed in stilling it, but I say why should it become stable? You have let your mind wander about all these days; I want this, I want this, and so on. Now you hope to make it still by merely asking your mind to keep quiet. How can that be possible?

---

4 Interruption; difficulties; false projection; tossing of the mind

911. 'I am unable to control my mind, what shall I do?' This is a general plaint. Give up worrying about the mind and offer *pranaam* saying, *'Aim Sri Guravae Namah'* or *'Guru Brahma Gurur Vishnu Guru Devo Maheshwaraha Guru Saakshat Para Brahma Tasmai Shri Gurave Namaha'*. Say it repeatedly and surrender to Guru. Then the mind will no longer be restless. While walking on the street, in the car on your way to the office, sitting in a chair in the office, when without work, repeatedly chant *'Gurur Brahma...'* this will enable you to get a hold over the mind.

912. You will have to engage the mind in something or the other, it will think of various things as soon as it has the opportunity, that's why keep it occupied in *puja*, reading scriptures, *japa*, meditation, chanting, *pranaam* etc. That's all. The mind won't have a chance to wander here and there.

913. To keep the mind in one's control, any Name of God, devotional song, poem, prayer or *japa* should be maintained on one's tongue.

914. Practice *manan* with the help of the mind. *Manan* means contemplation in solitude on what one has heard (about God). The short-cut to God in *Kali Yuga* is *manan* or *leela chintan*.

915. If the mind becomes restless while doing *japa*, chant *Naam* loudly till the mind becomes still. Once the mind becomes still, go back to *mantra japa*. After that, contemplate the divine sport of God. Chanting of God's Name and contemplating His divine sport, are simple paths one can adopt in this *yuga*.

Nature, Man & Health

916. The body, composed of five elements, is being destroyed every moment. By going for walks in open spaces, the loss of the sky is made good; through strolls in open air and inhalation of pure wind the loss of air is made good; through bathing and drinking of water, the water loss is made good; by rubbing mud on the body parts, loss of earth is made good and by dwelling regularly in the warmth of sunlight the loss of fire is made good.

917. *Yogasanas*, physical exercises approved by *yoga*, *mudras*[5] etc. are also extremely good. One should not exert in *pranayama* without Guru's instructions. *Baddha padmasana*[6] rids the body of diseases and awakens energy.

---

5 Gestures, which help to channel the flow of *prana* in the body
6 Bound lotus pose

Prana ~ Vital Breath

918. The *prana*[7] is straying in different directions today. The hue and cry is only because of it. The remedy? It is to control the *prana*. The way to control it is to restrain *rajas* and *tamas gunas*[8] and increase of *sattva guna*[9]. Enhancement of *sattva guna* is achieved through regular prayer and *japa* and eating pure food. Do not have the slightest doubt about the existence of God.

919. God is a firm principle. That is the reason; there is a need to have your mind and the breath still, in order to meet Him.

920. 72,72,10,201 arteries and veins make the *prana* vibrate in a *vikruta chanda*[10] and enslaves the individual to the senses, turning him into an animal. The majority of people today are bereft of *dharma*; even if the desire for *dharma* is awakened in anyone, the *prana* set to a *vikruta* vibration takes him away from this wish and leads him loyally to the sordid external pleasures wherefrom he has to undergo intolerable suffering.

---

7 Vital energy linked to breath
8 Modes of passion and inertia
9 Mode of purity and goodness
10 *Viruta/Vaikruta* : etymologically, change or transformation, inferring that which is 'derived from *Prakruti*'. The *Vikruta Chandas* refer to the transformation of the Ultimate Divine (*Brahman*) into the many-faceted world. In modern parlance, centrifugal forces.

Effects of Surya ~ Sun, on *Prana*

921. The heat of the sun destroys both disease and sins. He who worships the sun becomes free from sins swiftly. It is sin that obscures and obstructs attainment of knowledge. It is only after the sins have been destroyed that the knowledge of 'You are everything', springs up on its own.

922. The outer *prana* of every being is Surya. Due to the motion of the sun, the blood is polluted on full moon and new moon days. Illnesses like rheumatism are enhanced.

Paramanu Srishthi ~ Subtle Nature of Things

923. Another name of *paramanus*[11] is *prakriti*[12]. She is possessed of three *gunas*[13]. *Paramanu* and *prakriti* are not different.

924. All good and bad transactions of this world are done through *paramanus*. It is the *paramanus* that perform *leela*[14] in the form of human beings, animals, birds etc.

925. Whatever you are able to see is a manifestation of a collection of *paramanus*.

---

11 Subtle vibrations
12 Primordial Nature, which in association with Purusha, creates the universe.
13 *Sattva, rajas and tamas*
14 (Invisible) sport

926. The World-Mother is possessed of three *gunas*, and of the nature of great deluding potency, the wish-yielding tree; she sports in this world all-pervasively, assuming infinite states and forms-tastes-smells. Whenever an individual prays with the help of body, mind or sense organs, the Mother grants the object prayed for at that moment in the form of *paramanus*.

927. A man who repeats 'Ram, Ram', will attract the *paramanus* of Ram; where praise is being sung; there the Mother will send the *paramanus* of *stavan*[15]. As soon as the desire is awakened, the Mother sends forth *paramanus*. Ordinary men cannot grasp this, but *yogis* can harness these *paramanus* and demonstrate their presence.

928. As soon as anything is spoken or thought of, it attracts the *paramanus* of the nature of that object or person.

929. Evil deeds attract a host of foul *paramanus*. Wherever unfortunate activities transpire, the foul *paramanus* make it their home.

Flow of *Parmanus/ Sattvik Paramanus*

930. The *paramanus* of a *mantra* attract the *devatas*; in the same way the *paramanus* of man and woman attract each other.

---

15 Eulogies, hymns

931. By singing *Naam* aloud, the bad *paramanus* disperse –they are forced to run away.

932. Burning of aromatic fragrances, frankincense etc. attracts *sattvik paramanus*[16].

933. It is through the assemblage of *sattvik paramanus* that *Tulsi* and *Bilva* plants, *Peepal* and *Banyan* trees, are created. By worshipful service of the *Tulsi* or *Bilva* plant, and dwelling at their base, man becomes free of sins very quickly. By drinking *Tulsi* juice, man gains abundant *sattva guna*.

934. *Tulsi* (Holy Basil) is *sattva* personified. In *Tulsi* leaves, the *Tulsi* wood, the *Tulsi* fragrance, and in the soil at the root of a *Tulsi* plant, the quality of *sattva* is present in abundant measure. Service of *Tulsi* immerses the mind into *sattva* quality. The fragrance of *Tulsi*, entering through the nostrils, destroys the *tamas* (darkness) within, just as the external *tamas* is dispelled through the wind mixed with fragrance of *Tulsi*.

935. There is a singular and continuous relationship between Sri Hari and *Tulsi*. Remembrance of any one brings the other to mind. Lakshmiji may not always have stayed with Sri Hari, but *Tulsi Maharani* forever stays close to Sreenath.

---

16 Subtle vibrations

936. *Sattvik paramanus* stay unmoved and firm at places where there is well-wishing, noble thoughts and positive regard attributed to things; in these places *rajasic* and *tamasik paramanus*[17] are not allowed to enter and even if they do, they are drowned in *sattvik paramanus*.

937. All the *paramanus* of the group of rivers such as Ganga, Yamuna, Godavari, Saraswati, Narmada, Sindhu, Kaveri, and Krishna are *sattvik* in nature. By residing on the banks of these rivers, by drinking their holy water, a man is bound to acquire a *sattvik* nature.

938. In creatures like cows, deer and peacocks, and trees such as banana, mango etc., there are sufficient *sattvik paramanus*. In foods such as peas, lentils, *moong dal*, cow's ghee, and milk too, there are abundant *sattvik paramanus*.

939. Rosaries of *Tulsi*, *Rudraksha* and *Sphatik* enhance the property of *sattva*; *urdhvapundra*[18] or *tripundra*[19] attracts *sattvik paramanus*.

940. The touch of the *Shaligrama Shila*[20] can destroy sins of crores of lives; there is no rebirth, one gains proximity to Hari.

---

17 Subtle vibrations
18 Royal mark upon the forehead of Vaishnavites
19 Tripundra is a Shaivite's mark, three stripes of white vibhuti on the brow
20 Shaligrama is regarded as the symbol of Lord Vishnu.

Bhasma, Tilak Dharan & Shaligrama Paramanu

941. Smearing of *bhasma*[21] attracts *sattvik paramanus* and enhances the *sattva bhava* of the one who smears it.

942. *Rajas* and *tamas paramanus* cannot come close to those who smear all parts of their body with *bhasma*.

943. The *bhakta* can surely wear a *mala*[22] and *tilak*[23], declaring: 'I am a servant of God'. Making God an intimate associate, one can rid oneself of the attachment of body-consciousness.

944. When *Vaishnavas* apply *tilak* in *dvadash angas* (12 parts of the body), the mass of *sattvik paramanus* are attracted towards the *tilak* and unite where it has been smeared.

945. Through matted locks the *sattvik paramanus* are attracted and united in entirety; they strengthen the *sattva bhava* of the one with matted locks, progressively partaking of pure *sattva*, they transcend the *gunas*[24]. This is also the purpose behind wearing a *mala*.

---

21 Holy ashes from the sacrificial pit
22 Rosaries of *Tulsi*, *Rudraksha* etc.
23 Sacred mark (of a sandal) worn by *Vaishnavas* and *Shiavites* alike
24 Three human qualities: *tamas* (dullness & ignorance), *rajas* (energy & passion), *sattva* (harmony & purity)

946. The impure *paramanus* surround a sinner from inside and outside. He always dwells within the impure *paramanus* in sleep and in wakefulness.

947. One reaps a crore-time benefit by doing *japa* close to a *Shaligrama shila*.

948. *Mala, tilaka* etc. are identification marks of *dasatva* (servitude). By looking at the *tilak*, people recognize 'here is a servant of God', 'a traveller on the spiritual path'.

949. If you have a *tulsi* or *rudraksha mala*, wear it round the neck and do *japa*. Plant a *Tulsi* in a pot and keep the pot close to you when you do *japa*.

17

THE STATE OF *KUNDALINI* AWAKENING

950. Human beings need to worry only till the appearance of *Naad*. Once the Mother (*kundalini*[1]) is awakened, there is nothing to worry. The Mother floods our mind and *prana* in the musical sound of our being and dwells freely, sometimes sporting upwards, sometimes downwards.

951. The world of *Naad* is unprecedented. The *sadhaka* does not have the power to stop *Naad*. The Mother sports about and dances. The *sadhaka* is overwhelmed; he loses his mind and *prana*. He stands up, sits and sleeps like a machine, reads the *Shastras*; not an iota of his own influence is at work.

---

1 *Kundalini* is described as a sleeping, dormant potential force in the human organism. Many term it the serpent power because it lies coiled. It is one of the components of an esoteric description of man's 'subtle body', which consists of *nadis* (energy channels), *chakras* (psychic centres), *prana* (subtle energy), and *bindu* (drops of essence).

952. When the *kundalini* (serpent power) is activated, unbroken *Naad* (divine sound) goes on; it is beyond the powers of the spiritual aspirant to stop its momentum. *Naad Brahma* (Absolute in the form of Sound), sports sometimes in the higher and sometimes in the lower regions (spiritual centres of the body).

953. Awakening of the *kundalini* results in making all *mantras* instinctive with life (*mantra chaitanya*). This is an awakening that brings to light all the gods, secrets of mystic formulae (*mantras*), wisdom of the *Vedas*, and so on. The seeker is able to see all the deities and gain their grace. He or she becomes adept in all *mantras* and spiritual sciences, the mysteries of the *Vedas* are revealed.

954. When the spiritual aspirant forsakes all company and dwells in solitude, at that time *Naad* (divine sound) manifests in varied aspects. Whether the seeker listens to it or not, the Sound does not cease! Sometimes the (rumbling of) clouds, sometimes the (humming of) the bee, sometimes (chugging of) the engine, sometimes (gurgling of) the waterfall and sometimes (intoning of) '*Jai* Guru', or '*Om* Guru' or 'Guru Guru' – she plays in this manner.

955. The Mother (*kundalini*) sings and dances and destroys all our memory and *sanskaras*. *Naad* is the goal of all spiritual aspirants. The *Hathayogi* ultimately gains *Naad* and attains self-realization.

956. *Sadhana, bhajan*[2] etc. are not mere mental concepts; they are not figments of the imagination. There is unbounded joy in *sadhana* and *bhajan*; they liberate one from old age and death.

957. Texts composed in meters in Sanskrit, get the *prana* to vibrate in the *praakrut chanda*[3]. *Prana* is directed towards the *sushumna*[4] channel and one experiences great bliss. The bliss experienced after entering *sushumna* current is beyond words.

958. *Hathayogis* experience *Naad* after perfection of *Hathayoga*. Those who do *japa*, experience *Naad* in uninhabited places as they pursue their *japa*; those who are given to austerities, obtain *Naad* as a fruition of their practices. No matter which *sadhana* is adopted, the fruit is invariably *Naad*. *Kaaran Naad*[5] gives rise to *Omkar*, which gives rise to *Varna*[6], and the union of *varnas* gives rise to *bhasha*[7]. *Bhasha* is necessary for spiritual practice. Until *bhasha* ceases there can be no *siddhi*. *Bhasha* too ultimately merges with *Naad*.

---

2 Singing praise of God
3 *Praakruta* : etymologically, the original nature/state. Since the original state is the state of ultimate happiness (union with the Divine/*Brahman*), the *Praakruta Chanda* refers to those *Chandas*, which take the aspirant back to the original state of the ultimate happiness. In modern parlance, centripetal forces.
4 *Sushumna* is a *Naadi* in the human subtle body − one of the body's main energy channels that connects the base *Chakra* to the crown *Chakra*
5 Note of music *anahata* − the causal transcendental sound
6 Alphabet
7 Language

959. This is a secret the Gurus do not disclose. It is however imparted to deserving disciples; I am informing you of this because the common man today holds that God is a mental construct, and it is with the imagination alone that one can get onto the path of God. They feel that the blissful things of the external world don't exist within – that it's all arid inside. But this is not the case; there is an ocean of bliss within us. You don't have to imagine anything. One can experience transcendental sounds, touch, form, taste and smell within. By doing *japa* in a controlled manner, just for a few days, these come to light one by one.

960. There is no other path available to him who is walking the spiritual journey other than the path of *Jyoti* and *Naad*[8], which can bring about everything. Contemplating on *Naad*, the *yogi* merges with the unlimited, indescribable *Jyoti*. The *jnani* contemplates on *Naad* and becomes one with the supreme Brahma who is devoid of attributes. And as the *bhakta* contemplates on *Naad*, God comes and grants *darshan* (vision) to him. Whatever desires the supplicant has; by sitting beneath the wish-yielding tree of *Naam*, these desires are realized.

961. Those who worship *Jyoti* and *Naad* become worthy of being propitiated; they gain fame.

8 Divine sound and effulgence

962. Forsaking all activities and efforts, try with all your might to be one-pointedly absorbed in the *mantra*! Disease, sorrow, want, suffering will all flee. What will remain is happiness on earth, extremely delightful supreme bliss.

Hridaya Kamal ~ Lotus of the Heart[9]

963. Vyasadeva composed the *Bhagavata Purana* to bring peace to the heart. The heart is everything; once the heart is pleased, nothing else remains. When the heart has been stilled, it is one's duty to search for Hridayeshwar (Lord who resides in the heart), within one's own *hridaya* (heart).

964. Practice contemplating on the lotus in your heart. Again and again, try to concentrate the mind in the heart; several scriptures have unanimously espoused the heart centre.

965. When you meditate on the downward-faced lotus of the heart, it will face upwards. The lotus in the heart is characterized by eight-petals and is blood red. Orbs of the sun and moon, and fire, are in it. Seated in the centre is your *Ishta* (favourite deity). If you can't visualise it as such, concentrate only on the lotus.

966. Supreme bliss dwells in one's heart. As soon as one turns inwards, man finds the connection with that ocean.

---

9 Alludes to eight-petalled lotus *chakra*, called *Anahata*.

967. You return back to your own heart – then you will not need to go anywhere. Whatever you desire, you'll find it all in your own heart, all giving and receiving will transpire in the heart.

968. O devout disciples of Guru! You will find your *Ishta* and your Guru in your own heart. There is no need for you to stand outside and wail. Come into the heart! Your worldly desire of money is insignificant; even more trifling is your suffering on account of lust and anger! Come to the heart! You will experience the glory of your Lord even in the midst of your want, anger and lust.

Path of *Sushumna*[10]

969. **Disciple** Everything is *hamsa*, I realize.

Guru It is said in *Yoga Shruti,* The individual always does *japa* of the mantra *hamsa*. When *prana* (life) intensifies in the *sushumna* due to the activity of the *mantra* of the Guru, there is the reverse *japa* 'soham, soham, soham'. This is called *mantrayoga*. The realization of *mantrayoga* takes place in the western path (in the *sushumna* situated in the spinal cord).

970. *Ha-kara* is the sun, *sa-kara* is the moon, the unity of the sun and the moon is named *Hatha*. *Hathayoga* removes the inertia generated by all kinds of faults,

---

10 *Sushumna* is a *naadi* in the human subtle body – one of the body's main energy channels that connect the base *chakra* to the crown *chakra*

for in it the individual self becomes united with the Supreme Self. In this union the *chitta* (the mind) becomes absolutely calm.

971. **Disciple** Does the *bhakta* (the devotee following the path of surrender to God) realize '*soham*', 'I am that *Brahman*' etc?

   Guru God has said in the *Gita*: *Mamaivansho jivaloke jivabhuutah sanatanah*. The individual self is the part of *Brahman*. Where is the difficulty of realizing *soham*? Is not the spark of fire, fire? The power, *kundalini*, full of *nada*, gets awakened, sings '*soham, soham*' and sinks in the ocean of Absolute Bliss.

972. With the emergence of *Layayoga*, *prana-vayu*, vital breathing becomes absolutely calm. *Pranava*, the locus of bliss and infinite joy at the realization of the self which is the highest end, is derived from *layayoga*.

973. The *kundalini*, the great torch-bearer of energy to the path of God, moves to the *sahasrara*[11] through an extremely subtle channel; by adopting that course human beings enjoy perpetual health, supreme peace and loving devotion to God. When the motion of that current is checked, human beings suffer bondage, disease, sorrow, woes and torment. Man becomes an instrument of lust, anger etc. and leads his life akin to an animal.

---

11 *Sushumna* is a *naadi* in the human subtle body – one of the body's main energy channels that connects the base *chakra* to the crown *chakra*

True Realization

974. Until such time that an individual gains vision of God, he cannot have genuine peace.

975. My dear friend! Is it true you see Brahma all over? If that is the case, then why do you enjoy money and wealth, wife and son, clothes, and attendants, all by yourself? Why don't you distribute a part to the scavenger, who is also God? Go! Take part in his tiresome profession! Brahma is integrated and indivisible, right? If you have truly acquired knowledge of Brahma, the state of *advaita* (non-duality), how come you are wearing clothes? Why does Brahma need clothes? Why do you have a wife? Why does Brahma need a wife?

976. When *Naad* (celestial sound) and *Jyoti* (celestial light) manifest in the course of the devotee's practice, there arises in the heart of the aspirant an intense desire to have a vision of God, He forsakes everything. Then, as the contemplation on God, with exclusive devotion, continues, God cannot stay unmoved. He appears before the devotee in the manner in which He has been worshipped, and confers boons. The *mantra* of the spiritual aspirant merges into the favourite deity's person, and he is liberated.

977. For as long as such a devotee lives, in him the sound of *Omkar* plays from the *sushumna nadi* (the central

channel in the subtle body). Such people undertake the vow of accomplishing welfare of the world and live happily, exhausting their *prarabddha karma* (past *karmas* which have neared fruition), ultimately reaching the abode of eternal bliss. Whatever they behold – abodes terrestrial, aquatic or spatial; human beings, birds and beasts; insects, worms and moths – in these they witness only the play of God. Wherever the glance is cast, only Krishna is witnessed – the entire world becomes *Vasudevamaya* (divinity).

Discretion, Spiritual Powers & Experiences

978. While worshipping my beloved Krishna, my body has *romancha* (hair standing on end) and my mind filled with happiness derived from *bhakti*, tears have beautified my face and choked words sweeten my voice, I have at present not even a moment's leisure for other things. In this condition, all the four kinds of *mukti* (liberation), *salokya* (to stay near), *samipya* (to stay in front), *sarupya* (to have the same form) and *sajujya* (to become one with God), are standing at my gates, ready to serve me.

979. Consume *sattvik* food, study scriptural texts, and observe *brahmacharya*; every morning and evening contemplate your favourite deity in the lotus of your heart, and also mediate on the *mantra*, repeatedly inscribing it there; you will surely gain (spiritual) experiences soon.

930. One should not relate one's inner experiences to any Tom, Dick and Harry; speaking of it gives it away, it turns the experience into a malady.

981. Whether it is love, or anything else you like to name, it's not a thing to be displayed on the outside. Everything belongs within the heart. Keep it within.

982. With effort, a man can endeavour to engage himself in worship, meditation etc. in the wakeful state; however, if he is able to get a vision of God even in his dreams, it is the grace of God.

983. The future reveals itself during *japa*; it is not good to develop curiosity about it – it takes the person away from the goal of *japa* and enhances pride.

984. *Jyoti, Naad* and *Bindu*[12] are not figments of the imagination; they can be clearly seen and heard year after year.

985. There are crores of manifest and unmanifest *Naad*. These *Naad* and *Bindus* enable a man to have direct vision of God and be established in Him – man is drowned in divine bliss!

986. As soon as the *sattvika bhava* deepens, Jyoti and *Naad* appear. Gurudeva has asked me to follow the path of

---

12 Divine sound, effulgence, dot.

bhakti sadhan, whether I have *anubhuti* (experience) or not, I obey his orders and keep singing *Naam*. If one keeps chanting *Naam* with such determination, the *sattvika bhava* is bound to come. When the *sattvika bhava* deepens, it develops into *prema*. When *prema* appears, the whole universe becomes one with God.

987. Disease is destroyed first, then grossness is dispelled, thereafter with equable disposition Chandra (moon) incessantly rains down nectar. Fire, with the aid of wind, brings together all the bodily elements from all directions. Several types of *Naad* are initiated. The body becomes tender.

988. Pride and astonishment can both damage one's spiritual practice to a great measure. 'Can this happen to me?' This kind of astonishment is a defect.

989. What if you have yet to experience anything worth the name, such as *Naad, Jyoti, Bindu*, vision of deities etc. After all, you have your Guru. And as soon as you have Guru, you cease to be your narrow, little, limited caged self – indeed, your body, family property – all are Guru's. One is free the moment one sits at Guru's feet. Instantly, with initiation, comes emancipation. The purpose of *sadhana* is only to realize this great truth, to be just aware of this phenomenon.

Realization/s

990. First there is the *samsara bhava*, the worldly state; second one is *sadhak bhava*, seeker's state, third is the *jiva bhava*, state of soul's individuality and the fourth one is *ishvara bhava*, the state of divinity. It is only in the state of divinity that *dharma* can be established.

991. By dint of ascetic practice, when the mind and intellect becomes *vishuddha*[13], the *jyotirmaya atman*[14] is perceived by the mind intellect. This is called *atmadarshan* (revelation of the Self); the soul cannot be apprehended with the help of mortal eyes.

992. As soon as sins are destroyed, the complexion of an individual undergoes a change, it becomes bright and radiant. *Jyoti* shows through the body in the form of a halo. It is due to the concentration of *ojas*[15] secretion that *Jyoti* comes into being.

993. All agitations that come up during spiritual practice should be treated with the sentiment, 'Thou art everything!' and *pranam* should be offered to them with *ekarupa bahudhaa*[16]. At other times, men and women, birds and animals, moths and insects, every

---

13 Great purity that can enable visualization that may show event or entity at any place
14 Radiant mass of the Self
15 Vigour, strength and vitality, that is the essence of all tissues (*dhatus*), the sap of life, the essence of the immune system and spiritual energy
16 One in form, diversified into many

entity should be duly respected and saluted and addressed as 'It's Thee!' This is *anyarupa bahudhaa*[17].

Behaviour of the Emancipated

994. *Brahma-vijnani*, the knower of Supreme Reality, or *Ishvar-darshankari* (he who sees God), these do not need to abjure *karma*. In them *karma* drops off by itself.

995. Just as the body ceases to experience happiness and sorrow after death, he who is oblivious of happiness and sorrow while still alive, is worthy of attaining liberation.

996. He who is an imposter pretending to be a *jnani*, his posturing and parading can't last; people like this sometimes repeat 'money, money' and run after riches, and sometimes go after women seeking pleasures of the flesh, sometimes they pursue name and fame, ever running like dogs. They are a pain even to dogs and pigs.

997. After self-realization, when established in a state bereft of ignorance arising from duality, the sense of gender or the difference of experiencer and the experience is no longer prevalent. Thereafter, rules, ordinances, and proscriptions also do not remain.

---

17 In many other diverse forms

998. When by Guru's grace, Mother Kundalini wakes, she sets about breaking the three pitchers of *sthula*, *sukshma*, *karana deha*, one by one before she can merge in the Beloved.

999. The respectful disciple resorts first to Guru and Param Guru and throws himself heart and soul into spiritual exercise. When his reliance comes to be absolute, no longer can the Mother hold off, she has to wake up. It is she who unites the seeker with the Parameshthi Guru (God) and relieves him of the bondage of life.

1000. There is always a reward to honest effort. If thirst be there, my son, water will not be wanting. What is wanting is genuine thirst.

A DIVINE PROPHESY

'Listen to me again, oh you devotees of Krishna. In the district of Hooghly, a *bhakta* will be born in the family of devotees of Krishna. He will be known as a *Bengalee* because of his birth in Bengal. He will be vastly learned and attain to full knowledge of the Supreme and will be known as belonging to the Sri Sampradaya of the Rama-huti order. The cult of Sri Sampradaya of the Rama-huti order will be his daily practices. Vast will be his knowledge, meditation and learning. His disciples will number more than 1000. Of them about 300 will excel in knowledge and learning.

He will wander about from place to place to disseminate *dharma*. Many will receive from him the essence of truth. He will be dear to Sri Sri Jagannath Deva. He will be known to a good many wise men. As a householder, he will be known as Prabodh Chandra Mukhopadhyaya. From very early childhood he will possess knowledge as well as an attitude of non-attachment. At the second stage of life, he will have one leg damaged.

Wait, ye, for the advent of the Lord. In him will the Lord incarnate Himself. He will come on a visit to Niladrinath and his identity will be revealed. He will have many disciples with him and he will be forever wandering.'

A Divine Prophesy By Pandit Achyutanand, a leading sage of the Five Chosen Devotees and Scholars of Sri Krishna Chaitanya Mahaprabhu, 16th century Godhead.

ABHAY VAANI ~ Message of Hope

*Hare Krishna Hare Krishna Krishna Krishna Hare Hare
Hare Rama Hare Rama Rama Rama Hare Hare*

Devotee mine! You have no cause for fear. Chant only my Name. I am the fear of fear, the terror of the terrible. It is I who destroy all dangers. I have forever been protecting you. Oh dear! It is my duty to protect those who take my shelter with the words, 'I am yours!'

Let the skies topple down, let the Fire of dissolution play its havoc, let millions of thunders clash together, let the universe totter and reel and the fiercest of storms rage, let the seven seas swell and heave, yet-yet my dearest! You have no cause for alarm. Never forget that I have been guarding you right within my bosom.

Sita-Ram

CHANT THE NAME

Chant the Name… as you stand or sit, eat or go to bed, in weal and woe, in want as in affluence, devoutly or disdainfully, with or without reverence, in solitude as well as in company, awake and asleep, chant my Name.

I say on oath I undertake full responsibility for you and your family. You need not worry about anything whatever.

JAI GURU

In the higher approaches, there is no difference between the various *Sampradayas* (spiritual orders). Though some outer differences may be visible, in reality all are the same.

The *mantra* of the union of all the *Sampradayas* (spiritual orders) is *Jai Guru*. To whichever *Sampradaya* a person may belong, he has to take shelter with a Guru; hence, with great *ananda* (rejoicing), he will not be shy at announcing, 'Victory to Guru Deva!'

The meaning of the words *Jai Guru* is 'Victory to Guru Deva!' Sri Gurudeva is everything to me; so if he is victorious I certainly shall be fulfilled.

The syllable 'gu' denotes darkness or ignorance; the syllable 'ru' stands for the repeller of darkness.

NAAM DHARMA

Hare Krishna Hare Krishna Krishna Krishna Hare Hare
Hare Rama Hare Rama Rama Rama Hare Hare

The Name is the quintessence of all *mantras*: this is the
purport of all the *Shastras*.

The Name of Hari,
The Name of Hari,
The Name of Hari alone:
There is no other way in this degenerate Age!

RAMANANDIYA SRI VAISHNAVA JAI GURU SAMPRADAYA PARAMPARA

Sri Kakustha Sriram Ji
Sri Sita Ji
Sri Vishvaksen Ji
Sri Shathakop Swamiji
Sri Nathmuni Ji
Sri Pundarikshaaksha Muni Ji
Sri Ram Mishra Ji
Sri Yamunacharya Ji
Sri Mahapoornacharya Ji
Sri Ramanujacharya Ji
Sri Kuresh Swami Ji
Sri Madhavacharya Ji
Sri Bopdev Ji
Sri Devadhipaacharya Ji
Sri Purushottamacharya Ji
Sri Gangadharacharyaa Ji
Sri Rameshwaracharya Ji
Sri Dwaranandacharya Ji
Sri Devanandacharya Ji

Sri Shriyanandacharya Ji
Sri Haryanandacharya Ji
Srimad Raghavanandacharya Ji
Sri Jagatguru Bhaashyakaar
Sri Madramanandacharya Ji
Sri Anantanand Ji
Sri Ganesh Ji
Sri Purnavairati Ji
Sri Kaludas Ji
Sri Gangadas Ji
Sri Vishnudas Ji
Sri Harbhanjandas Ji
Sri Ghanshyamdas Ji
Sri Prayagdas Ji
Sri Lakshmandas Ji
Sri Bhaktamali Ramdas Ji
Sri Madhavdas Ji
Shrimad Damodardas Ji
Shrimad Dasharathidev Yogeshwar Ji
Sri Sitaramdas Omkarnath Ji

AFTERWORD

I completed the first draft of the translation of *Omkarsahasravani* in 1999. Unfortunately, the manuscript was lost and I had to redo it entirely. A few months after this, once again, a part of it was destroyed inadvertently in a café. Even though it was one of the earliest manuscripts to be completed, it remained unpublished for nearly a decade due to some whim of destiny. Perhaps the time was not right. Perhaps He did not will it.

Finally, when the first edition was brought out in 2008, as *Cloudburst Of A Thousand Suns*, sponsored in the memory of the Late Vellanki Murali Mohan Rao, as service at Guru's feet, Tridandi Swami Sri Madhav Ramanuj Jeeyar was delighted. He had in the meanwhile entrusted me with the job of editing the second volume *of Omkarsahasravani*. I pointed out to him the parts of the second volume which were repetitive. He replied that it has been written the way it has 'come' and I should work on it the way it 'comes' to me. I did. The book, as it stands in its present form, includes *vaanis* from both volumes of *Omkarsahasravani*, and at least a dozen other kindred texts by Sri Sitaramdas

Omkarnath, such as *String of Pearls, Mad Man's Wallet, Brahmanusandhan, Pranav Prem Piyush Bhashya* of the *Gita,* Sri Sri Naadleelamrit and Naamamrit Lahari.

I would like to thank Kishore Rao, for initiating the idea of publishing the first edition of this book and A N Chatterjee, who had been working on the text simultaneously, though my rendering was completed faster than his. I exchanged notes with him and profited much from it. I thank Swarup Nanda, the publisher and Chandralekha Maitra, the editor, who took great pains to shape the book into its present form; Dr Arindam Chakrabarti, for allowing me to hold him captive in Rishikesh Ashram until his preface was done, and Amarendra Athalye and Shreepad Bopardikar, for being of assistance financially so that the book could become affordable and reach more and more people.

The masterly prefaces at the beginning of this text by Kinkar Vitthal Ramanuja, Madhav Swami and Dr. Arindam Chakrabarti, have said everything that must be said of this text; I can only add this from my personal experience: Sri Sitaramdas Omkarnath's soul is invested in this text, he speaks through these words and for this reason it is indeed a living gospel.

Raj Supe
(Kinkar Vishwashreyananda)